Babies are the Worst

A Memoir about Motherhood, PPD, & Beyond

Meagan Gordon Scheuerman

Cover design: Kelsey Cross
Cover photography: Kelsey Cross

This book is memoir. It reflects the author's present recollections of experiences over time. Some names and characteristics have been changed, some events have been compressed, and some dialogue has been recreated.

The advice and strategies found within may not be suitable for every situation. This work is sold with the understanding that neither the author nor the publisher are held responsible for the results accrued from the advice in this book.

www.meaganscheuerman.com

OQ Books
First Edition

Contents

For anyone who has thought this title.

You are not alone.

Introduction

Hello.

"Tell me about yourself."

A common job interview prompt. Whether for a regular 9 to 5 gig or in a meeting with a casting director.

And just there I've told you a little about myself.

Hi. My name is Meagan and I'm an actor, writer, mother. In that order, chronologically. But, you know, "not in that order."

"Oh? You're an actor? What have I seen you in?"

Commercials. You've seen me shilling for restaurants and cars, airlines and chips. Brown hair, brown eyes, a friendly smile? Remember me? Of course you don't and that's totally fine. I have the kind of face that blends in so you won't remember me too much, which is surely why I was cast in these spots. They wanted you to remember the product I was advertising, instead of the gal in the commercial. I'm a bit of an "every" woman. People always tell me I look "just like" their cousin/sister/friend/aunt. In NYC, I was once headed into a casting and a woman stopped me on the front steps of the building. "Hey, Meagan! How are you??" And she gave me a big ol' hug. I awkwardly hugged back and said, "I'm so sorry, do I know you?" And she was like, "Meagan Blahblahblah?" And I was like, "No...Meagan Gordon." That's how unremarkable I look. There's even another MEAGAN walking around out there with my same face. Enough to warrant a hug. I wish I could remember the last name of this other Meagan/Meghan/Megan/Meaghan. I would totally look her up. Odd mix-ups aside, I learned to embrace my universal look. Commercials are how I got my SAG card and I was glad to have the work.

When I moved to LA, I auditioned as much as I could but there was also a writer's strike happening so work was scarce. I ended up putting my English degree from the University of Florida to use and started working part-time as a copywriter for an internet marketing company. I also helped maintain one of their blogs. So beyond my own personal blogging efforts, I was actually paid to write. I became a writer.

When the strike ended jobs were still scarce and I realized I was getting older. A decade went by and suddenly I was in my 30s and I thought, why am I waiting to start a family? Acting will always be there. My window for motherhood will continue closing.

So I got pregnant, had a baby, and became a mother in 2013.

And then I got depressed.

I never saw it coming.

This is my story about postpartum depression.

This is *not* the book I thought I'd be writing one day.

Postpartum depression was something that happened to other women. Not to me. It wasn't even on my radar of possibilities. And yet nine months after giving birth, I knew something wasn't right. Ten months after my son was born, I finally talked to someone. Eleven months after he was born, I went on medication.

None of these were easy decisions. Certainly not ones I thought I'd ever have to make.

This is my story about how I got there.

And how I ended up here.

* * * * *

If you're pregnant and you think postpartum depression won't happen to you, I can relate. But unlike me, you have the chance to prepare for the 8-19%[1] chance that it does. If that percentage seems low, that's because it is. That's the *reported* number of diagnosed postpartum depression cases. In reality, nearly one million women[2] each year experience some form of perinatal mood or anxiety disorder. If you're a new mom wondering if things will get better, you should read this so you know you're not alone. If you're a "seasoned" mom and you remember how hard it can be, you should read this so you know you weren't alone. If you're a spouse whose

---

[1] cdc.gov

[2] http://postpartumprogress.org/the-facts-about-postpartum-depression/

wife is expecting, you should read this so you know what signs to look for. If you're a new parent wondering if your wife is ever going to stop crying, you should read this so you can be a better partner. If you're a mom whose new motherhood experience was a breeze, you should read this so you know how lucky you are and what your friends or loved ones may be going through.

A well-meaning, totally wise friend reached out to me when I was a few weeks from delivering. She said, "You should read about postpartum depression just in case. It happened to me and if I knew what to look for, I may have gotten help sooner." I thanked her. . .and didn't take her advice. I kept trucking along in my naive bubble. I didn't understand the nature of depression. I thought that I would be okay for several reasons:

1. Becoming a mom was a dream coming true. I couldn't wait to meet my son. We had planned and tried for him. He was the puzzle piece that would complete our family portrait.

2. I'd never been depressed and from what I had heard, you were more likely to get postpartum depression if you had struggled with "regular" depression in the past.

3. My pregnancy had been a breeze so I had no doubt delivery would follow suit.

Pride cometh before the fall.

I've learned that depression does not discriminate.

I've also learned that the statistics reported on the number of women who experience postpartum depression (8-19%)[3] versus how many women are *suspected* to experience postpartum depression (1 out of 7) differs vastly. [4]. According to the American Psychological Association, "*PPD can affect any woman—women with easy pregnancies or problem pregnancies, first-time mothers and mothers with one or more children, women who are married and women who are not, and regardless of income, age, race or ethnicity, culture or education.*" So, um, basically ANYONE. Thanks for clearing that up, APA.

---

[3] cdc.gov

[4]apa.org

Postpartum depression is the most common "disorder" associated with pregnancy and childbirth that we hear about as a society, but it isn't the only postpartum mood disorder that exists. Other postpartum issues include postpartum anxiety (PPA), postpartum post traumatic stress disorder (PPTSD), postpartum OCD (PPOCD), bipolar mood disorder, and postpartum psychosis. [5] Hmm, maybe they should up that 1 out of 7 estimate to include all of the forms of postnatal complications that can come up. And if they did that, I bet the estimate would be closer to 6 out of 7 women who experience some kind of postpartum disorder - this based on my small swath of personal encounters. I have yet to meet a new mom who isn't struggling in some way to find her balance again. And I'm not just talking about those first sleep-deprived weeks when you're adjusting to having a new baby at home. Symptoms of postpartum depression can show up anytime *during* pregnancy or in the *first twelve months after* childbirth.

---

[5] postpartum.net

Such statistics aren't exclusive to new moms, either. That rollercoaster of hormones coursing through their veins isn't always the only factor. Let's not forget about the other half of the equation - the dads or partners. Approximately 4% of fathers experience depression within the first year of childbirth. Nearly 21% will experience depression by the time their child is 12 years old [6]. We are societally conditioned to show the "good" side of becoming a parent. So for instance, the lack of sleep you experience as a new parent is often portrayed as a badge of honor. When in reality, "the consequences of sleep deprivation at 24 hours is comparable to the cognitive impairment of someone with a blood-alcohol content of 0.10 percent, according to a 2010 study in the International Journal of Occupational Medicine and Environmental Health." [7]. My theory? Cumulative lack of sleep is as much of a contributing factor to postpartum depression as hormonal fluctuations. And that is going to affect our partners, too.

---

[6] cdc.gov

[7] everydayhealth.com

But at the end of the day, what I've learned is to forget the statistics and the theories. Forget all of that. Because the common thread to all of this is that *parenthood is hard.* And it's not always fun. Or blissful. Or easy. Sure, there may be moments of fun or bliss or ease. But it can be downright, shockingly difficult. And that's true whether you are experiencing a postnatal mood disorder or not. So this book is about all of that, too. It's about recognizing your emotions as a new parent, and giving value to them. I wasn't diagnosed with postpartum depression until ten months after Owen was born. I didn't seek help until then. Which means that for the beginning, while I was in the thick of it, I didn't have the help I needed. And I just had to keep trudging on. And so often, that's what women do. They don't seek the help they need because they also need to keep a little human alive.

And who has the time to think about anything beyond that?

Part One:

My PPD Journey

Chapter 1

Motherhood: Always in the Plan

I've been thinking a lot about life narratives. How our sense of self grows from the stories of how we came into the world. This is how my narrative goes:

I was born to an audience.

Seriously.

When my mother gave birth there was a team of medical students observing my entrance. The story goes that applause erupted when I came screaming forth. Apparently the birth was "textbook" in its execution. Exactly how a typical birth should go. And so it's no wonder that I wanted to be an actress for as long as I can remember. How could I not after that debut? And it's no wonder that I've always had a need to please, to be perfect, to be what is expected because that's how I started with my very first breaths: I gave the med students what they wanted. "Let me entertain you, let me make you smile..." Oh, *Gypsy*.

Those are lyrics to a musical I'll never forget. When I was ten years old I auditioned for a local high school production of *Gypsy*. They needed child actors to play the younger versions of the main characters. I had to sing that song for the role of Baby June. I was convinced that I was a shoo-in. Why wouldn't I be? Confidence was something I rarely lacked at ten. That was until I saw the high school student playing the adult version of June. I was taller than her. There goes my chance at the part. At ten years old I was a bit of a mutant. I'm quite an average height now but I got to this average much sooner than most. I peaked early and then was stunted. Perhaps that's the story of my life . . .

My pregnancy with Owen was textbook. Actually, it was better than textbook. We decided to officially start trying to get pregnant after returning home from a cruise with our extended family. I'd been using the "Period Tracker" app to monitor my cycles for a few months and I was supposed to be 'fertile' when we got home. If you're not familiar with the app, you put the day your period starts and ends into a calendar and then it calculates the average length of your cycle to give you a range of dates that you might be ovulating. On the dates that you're fertile, a green dot shows up on the calendar. On the day of ovulation, a little flower icon pops up. Green light means go, so we gave those days our best shot. When I was six days out from starting my next period, I took an early detection test. The second line was so faint, I almost missed it. But it was there. I took another test two days later and the line was darker. We got pregnant with Owen the first time we tried. I wouldn't know how rare and lucky that was until we decided to try for another child a few years later. But that's another story. We'll get there.

I wasn't sick for a single day during my pregnancy with Owen. I had an aversion to red meat but never had morning sickness, queasiness, or loss of appetite. I ate healthier than I ever had in my life, paying close attention to what I was feeding my child and myself. I stayed active with regular hikes, long walks, and a pregnancy workout DVD. I was determined to never feel "handicapped" by my pregnancy and even oh-so-humbly-bragged about that conviction on the mommy blog that I started after finding out I was pregnant. Let's just say I was pretty naive and overconfident through my entire pregnancy. Kind of like when I was ten and auditioned for *Gypsy,* only to discover I was "too big for my britches." I was building myself up for a far fall.

* * * * *

Already the mythology of my son Owen's life is taking shape. He was born with his eyes wide open. This is a strange phenomenon since most babies wait a few minutes until after birth to open their eyes and most don't open their eyes fully until an hour or so after birth. But when my doctor finally cut me open so he could get out (more on that later), she said he was looking right at her. He was "sunny side up," which is partially why he was stuck to begin with. He was literally lying, face up, eyes open, waiting. Throughout his infancy we continually heard, from strangers and friends alike, that he was, "So alert!" I didn't understand it at first. Alert how? What did that mean? But then I started observing other babies his age and I understood. Owen looked right at you. He still does. He locks eyes like he is engaging in an internal dialogue with you - asking questions and making observations and comments. He looks around his surroundings and notices anything new or different immediately. He spoke with his eyes before he could possibly know language. Other babies his age always appeared unfocused. Their eyes may have been open but they weren't *seeing*. Owen could be a bit unnerving because you could tell that he saw you. It was like he looked through you and saw to the other side.

Which only made my shame feel that much deeper.

I have always wanted to be a mother. There was never a doubt in my mind whether or not motherhood was in my future. One of the adjectives tossed about in my narrative has always been "maternal." My mom always commented on how I was a "natural" with children, especially with babies. I started babysitting my newborn sister when I was nine years old. I took care of neighborhood children when I was ten. I looked older than I was and I acted older. I played mother to my friends, making sure everyone felt comforted and supported and nurtured. I cultivated my maternal instincts; there was a definite pride there.

The summer I graduated from high school I was a camp counselor at a sleepaway camp. I worked with the middle school kids and loved when some of my campers started calling me "Mama Meagan." They even made a nametag for me with that alliterative title. If they felt homesick or scared, I would help them feel better. I'd sing them to sleep or make them laugh in spite of their homesickness, and I reveled in my role. I continued to work with children throughout college, as a tutor to elementary students, and as a play leader at a play space called O2B Kids. I volunteered as a BookPAL through the SAG (Screen Actors Guild) Foundation while living in Los Angeles because as my birth debut suggested, I would become an actress. My pursuit led to jobs, which led to union status, which led to a position to "give back" to the community. And the community I always felt most at ease with was children. In one of the third grade classes I read to, there was a little boy who always sat at the front of the rug while I read. He'd practically sit on my feet. One day, completely out of the blue, he said, "I wish you were my mom." I swelled up like a peacock. My vanity knows no bounds. Picture me fists raised, like a boxing champ, bouncing from foot to foot, crowing, "I'M EVERY MOTHER!" I may not be able to do a lot of things but motherhood, man, that was going to be a breeze. I mean, even this little kid who sees me for thirty minutes each week can sense how awesome a mom I'm going to be. Brush that shoulder off.

I knew in my bones that I was *ready* to be a mom all along, but when would the *right* time be? Being an actor put a few restrictions on my timeline. Dan and I married by the time I was twenty-five. Checkmark for my "life plan." You know, the life plan you make when you're in high school and clueless? I figured my timeline would be as follows:

1. Become a world-famous actress in my early twenties.

2. Get married by twenty-five.

3. Start having babies two years later.

4. Live happily ever after.

My third check mark kept getting pushed back because my first check mark hadn't quite panned out. As my twenties ticked by, my career still wasn't at the point I had expected, or at least hoped, it would be. So I didn't want to get pregnant just yet. I mean, what if that perfect role came along and I was pregnant and couldn't snag it? You know, the role that would make all my dreams come true? I was convinced that it was out there and I didn't want to risk screwing it up by being knocked up. So I kept trucking along - going on auditions, going to casting workshops, doing mailings to casting agencies, following up with my agents regularly to see if things were slow all over or just for me. Hustle hustle hustle. I was running faster and faster on that hamster wheel, tricking myself into believing I was making progress. But each year passed with more close calls and near misses. I screen tested for a major role on a soap opera, but didn't get the part. I was on hold for big national commercials, only to be released. A casting workshop would go really well and I'd be convinced that the casting director would call. But they never did. And before I knew it, I was staring thirty in the face. And what did I have to show for it? Some commercials and a hot husband. No small feat, admittedly, and not that it wasn't enough. But it wasn't. I wanted to start a family with Dan and waiting for that "perfect" role much longer felt like a cruel delay. I always knew my perfect role was to be a mom so what was I waiting for?

It was time to flip the script.

Chapter 2

Under the Sea

On most actors' resumes, you'll see a "special skills" section tacked on at the end. It's usually a list of unique qualifications so that if a role calls for a special talent, casting can find you. If a role requires someone that is a proficient equestrian, this is where you can get your edge. Do you speak five different languages? Put it here. If you are a hula-hooping champ, put it down. You never know! Actors cultivate skills like karate and knitting and foreign accents to get a leg up on the competition. *Fingers-crossed* someday your knife-throwing skills will come in handy. And if you know how to do something a little beyond the norm, all the better. You can list your skill *and* come to auditions armed with a fun conversation starter if the casting team is inclined to ask. So what's my fun little quirk? I'm a skin diver with the added bonus of being an "expert with a tickle stick." It all sounds so salacious, doesn't it? Sex sells! Though this skill has nothing to do with sex, most casting directors don't have any idea what skin diving is or how to use a tickle stick. But the names are enough to pique their interest. I've had plenty of casting directors and agents raise an eyebrow and ask, "What exactly is a 'tickle stick'?" And that's when I get to explain that a tickle stick is a straight metal rod with a curved end that divers use to "tickle" lobsters out a hole so we can catch them in a net. Sexy, right?

For the better part of my life, my family has rented a house in the Florida Keys during the last week of July to participate in lobster mini-season. Official hunting season for Florida lobster begins in August, but every last Wednesday and Thursday of July, the season opens for two days to non-commercial fisher-people. And that's us! We head down with decades of knowledge about the directional coordinates of lobster holes, ready for the hunt. If the weather cooperates, we can spot these holes from the boat. We'll throw out a weighted marker buoy and dive in to check out the inventory. But if the weather isn't completely clear with zero wind, which is more often the case, we'll drag behind the boat. We attach a ski rope to the back hooks and then the captain (ahem, my dad) drives the boat slowly around an area as we look at the sandy ocean floor, hoping to see something promising.

When you spot a hole and dive down to inspect, the world slows down. You hear the glubglubglub of your snorkel pushing out air and filling with water. Your limbs move slower against the water than they do against air. You hold your breath for an eternity as you inspect the number of lobster antennas you see. Then you poke your tickle stick in the hole and hope you don't disturb an eel or a nurse shark, who also like to take up residence in large lobster holes. Your lungs start to burn and your heart starts to race after you've been under too long and you kick yourself slowly back to the surface so you can breathe again. What seemed like an eternity has been all of 45 seconds.

And there it is.

That sensation is what being depressed feels like. At least for me.

I was underwater, floating through my life, lungs slowly starting to ache, unable to breathe. I couldn't react as quickly as I expected. Depression muffled my perception of life the way water muffles sound. The highs and lows of motherhood were muted. I didn't feel overwhelmingly sad. I just felt an overwhelming amount of nothingness. I would go through the motions but not the *emotions*. And that was something that surprised me. And also why I didn't think of myself as depressed for such a long time. I always perceived depression as overwhelming sadness. But I *wasn't* sad. I was under the sea. This was how my therapist helped to determine my diagnosis. She said that one of her first questions for patients that come in with suspected depression is, "Are you sad?" If their answer is yes, she says, "Good! Chances are you aren't depressed!" And people are like, "Huh? This lady is a quack." They're surprised. I was surprised. The tricky thing about depression, she explained, is that it's not the presence of sadness that determines it. It is the *absence* of emotion. Depression is the *suppression* of normal human emotions.*

And when you feel nothing, you have nothing to live for. And when there is nothing to live for, there is nothing to lose if you're gone.

Depression is a vicious liar.

* *Important to note that the above information from my doctor was specific to me and my diagnosis.* **Depression can look different on everyone.** *To give us a broader understanding of some of the more clinical issues addressed in this book, Dr. Abigail Levrini, acclaimed psychologist and author, will provide us with "Doctor Notes" as we go along.*

Chapter 3

The Hardest Cry

Immediately after I gave birth, I knew something was wrong. They cut me open, took Owen out and I didn't want to look at him. I didn't care. I was so, so tired both physically and mentally that I just wanted to close my eyes and sleep forever. But that wasn't how I was supposed to feel, that wasn't the movie version. I was supposed to look at him and feel the most beautiful, powerful love I'd ever experienced. A love beyond understanding. There should have been angels singing, announcing that true love had arrived. Not the case. The doctors swept Owen away to be examined and get medical clearance first thing. They may have held him up for me to see, but I also may have imagined that moment. Because I don't remember the first time I saw him. I do remember the first time I held him. Because I put on a show. They brought him over, and as I held him, I laughed and smiled and did the things that I had seen in movies and on TV. I figured that was what was expected of me. I stared into Owen's all-knowing eyes and continued to coo my hellos and thought, "Why don't I feel anything?"

That feeling, or lack thereof, went beyond the emotional. Because I had been shaking so badly before the surgery, I literally couldn't feel my arms. As in, my arms were totally asleep. When Owen was placed in my arms for the first time, I just remember a heavy feeling. You know when a limb falls asleep and you can poke it and it feels like a hunk of meat, unattached yet attached to yourself? That's the feeling I had in that first encounter. Owen's seven pounds felt like a seventy-pound weight on my chest. My mind and my body were, quite literally, numb.

Once the doctors and nurses had cleaned us both up, it was time to transfer to the recovery room. They propped this ginoromous weight of a baby on my chest and nestled him in the crook of my arm. I felt panic. He was going to slide out of my dead arms on the way down the hall. There was no way I'd be able to hold him and keep him safe during the transfer. As the nurses arranged him in my arms, I asked, "Can't Dan hold him?" The nurses exchanged a concerned look. One asked, "You don't want to hold your baby?" Her tone clearly sounded worried. Which pissed me off!! Don't shower me with pity and concern, lady. It's not that I don't want to hold him — I don't want to kill him! I snapped back, "Of course I do! But my arms are asleep. I'm afraid I'll drop him." They exchanged that look of concern again. How dare they?! The other said, "You won't drop him. Don't worry." I felt dismissed. Don't worry?? I wanted to scream, "You don't know that!!! You don't know anything!!! And stop looking at me like something is wrong with me because I don't want to hurt my baby! Or have anything to do with him!" If I relived this moment now, having been through PPD, I would join those nurses in the look of concern. Instead I shut down, swallowed my sobs and let the heaviness of it all lay on my chest, along with my sweet baby, as they pushed me to the recovery room. I was too tired to do anything else.

It was when we were in the recovery room that I stopped swallowing the sobs. I was trying to breastfeed for the first time and Owen wasn't really able to latch. I thought maybe if I sang it would relax us both. I started to sing, "Hush little baby don't say a word, Mama's gonna buy you a mockingbird . . ." and my voice cracked. Suddenly I was crying and I couldn't stop. I tried to keep singing through the tears; I'm certain I sounded like a lunatic. Singing to my baby for the first time was too much for me to handle. Maybe that sounds like a typical reaction, that singing to your baby to help calm him for the first time is a big event. And feeling emotional about it is nothing to be concerned about. But these weren't tears of joy. An immense sorrow was starting to creep into the corners of my heart. Water was starting to seep under the door. All of a sudden, I was in complete denial that I had a baby. I couldn't reconcile the actual events with my imagined version, the version of how it was "supposed" to happen. So the fact that I was singing to my baby for the first time didn't compute. And why did I pick that song? Is that what I really wanted to sing for the first time to Owen? No. Did I actually have a "first song" picked out? No. But he was crying and I wanted him to hush. And I wanted to eat. Oh my god why won't they just let me eat?

That's when the tears started.

* * * * *

On our way home from the hospital, my crying reached its peak — near hysteria. It started as I was being wheeled out. Sitting in my wheelchair, rolling down the incredibly long maternity ward hallway I started sobbing. This was not how anything was supposed to go. There were women with family and friends in their hospital rooms and people waiting in the visitors' room outside the doors. We had no one. And I suddenly realized what a mistake that was. Friends had called after I delivered and asked when they could come visit in the hospital. I told them not to come. I couldn't put on a happy face for everyone. Our family was still on the other side of the country, per our request, so we could have time to "get settled" as a family. And what were we doing leaving with a baby? I wasn't ready. I had made a mistake by having a baby. I was trying to smile. I was trying not to cry as hard as I was crying. But I was gasping for air. The nurse didn't say anything. She didn't ask if I was ok. But that didn't matter because even if she had, I would have said that I was fine and blamed the sobbing on the hormones. In fact, I'm guessing she saw this type of crying enough not to ask.

"Baby blues" affects 70-80 % of new mothers and usually hits between four and five days after birth[8]. However, depending on the circumstances of the birth, it can show up earlier. The first symptom listed about baby blues on the American Pregnancy website: "Weepiness or crying for no apparent reason." So if 8 out of 10 of us are crying "for no reason" within a few days of giving birth and a typical hospital stay for a caesarean is three days, I'd guess nurses are quite accustomed to just letting new mothers "cry it out" as we roll away to our cars. The weepiness/irritability/insomnia/

---

[8] americanpregnancy.org

anxiousness/sadness known as "baby blues" is the body's response to the flood and fluctuation of hormones after giving birth. It tends to last for a few weeks as the body acclimates to this major life change — that whole bringing a human into the world thing. Yes. I expected to experience them. No. I did not expect to feel so absolutely out of control.

Once we were in the car, I stopped trying to control the crying. I sat in the backseat next to Owen and broke down into a hysterical mess. Dan asked what was wrong, but I didn't know. I couldn't explain it. I was experiencing the deepest level of grief that I had ever felt. It wasn't something I could articulate. So Dan just let me cry.

When we walked in the door to our apartment I collapsed.

I wasn't ready.

When we left for the hospital on Friday night, I did not think for a second that we would be returning on Tuesday with a baby. I wanted to labor at home, go for walks around the neighborhood, stopping and holding onto Dan as a contraction came on. I wanted to bounce on my exercise ball and breathe through the pain. It's astounding to look back now at how important that narrative was to me. Becoming a mother was a journey, and I had a path plotted for my journey.

By the time I returned home, I was miles away from my plan.

Chapter 4

Labor & Delivery

This is how I thought it would go down:

I would slowly and naturally go into labor. There would be the excited "This is it!" moment where twinges of pain are realized as labor pains. We live a mile from the hospital so I'd tough it out in the comfort of my home, using my breathing techniques and labor ball and husband for support. We'd go on a walk; I'd take a bath; I'd listen to relaxing music; I'd time carefully. When contractions were 4 to 5 minutes apart for an hour, we'd head to the hospital. If I decided I needed meds, I'd get them. Then I'd deliver my baby naturally. I'd see him enter the world and in a moment of euphoria I'd remember forever, he'd be placed on my chest, all gooey and fresh, for skin-to-

skin bonding time. We'd weep with joy and be overwhelmed with love.

None of that happened.

Here is what did.

* * * * *

I woke up around 6:00AM on Friday, Feb. 22, which was pretty standard. We were living in LA but my husband works for a company on the east coast, so that's when his day started. Since his office was in our bedroom (because the nursery took over his office), I always got up when he did and moved into the nursery so I could get a little more sleep. But on this particular morning I had some slight cramping. It was nothing severe, but enough to have to breathe consciously through it. Since I was two days past my due date I got a little excited. Maybe this was it! Since the cramping was minor, I tried to fall back asleep and about a half hour later, the cramps were back. This could be it! Again, I tried to fall back asleep. Everything I had read said that in early labor, try to rest and relax. Once labor started getting more intense, sleep was going to be scarce. But about a half hour later, the cramps came back again. I went back into our bedroom and told Dan I was having some cramps at about half hour intervals. He packed his bag. We waited for the next one. A half hour passed. Then another thirty minutes. Then another. Then nothing else happened. The cramps were gone. We felt a little deflated, but encouraged that *something* seemed to be happening. My cousin and his wife had their c-section scheduled for the 22nd and it was exciting to think that our children might share a birthday.

* * * * *

I went about my day and noticed that I was leaking some fluid. I put on a panty liner and it didn't get soaked so I assumed that the fluid was urine. The baby was definitely sitting low and I thought he might be pushing on my bladder, causing some incontinence. I also noticed some sloughing off of something every time I urinated.

But since my doctor had swept my membranes on Wednesday, I assumed that the residue I saw was a result of that. When a doctor sweeps your membranes, they do a manual finger sweep of your cervix, a process that, in theory, helps separate the membranes of your cervix from the amniotic sac. The hope is that the hormones released help stimulate natural labor. It's an actual physical scraping (slightly painful, as you can imagine) so residue is expected. The residue I was seeing was light brown, so I figured what I was seeing was related to the sweep. The cramps I had in the morning were now gone and whatever was leaking was so slow that I didn't need to change my panty liner for hours. False alarm — I thought.

A friend stopped by in the afternoon and I remembered joking that, "Who knows? I might be in labor right now and not realize it." She laughed and said, "I'm pretty sure you'll know when you're in labor." This was around 2:00PM. I had a few more cramps during the day but nothing consistent, and nothing that lasted longer than a few seconds. I figured it was Braxton Hicks.

Dan and I made a steak dinner around 6:30; big steak, baked potato and a salad. My cousin had just had her baby. I hadn't had any more signs of labor. We started eating and I made a toast with my water : "Hope to see you again later, Steak." I'd read that most women vomit from the pain of labor. It was a joke. At least, I thought it was a joke.

As we finished dinner, I felt a rush of fluid. More than I had felt throughout the day. I went to the bathroom to check things out and noticed that the fluid now had a pinkish tinge. Hmm . . . maybe I should call the doctor? This might not be pee after all.

The doctor on call listened impatiently to me. "I'm 40 weeks, 2 days, and I've been leaking some sort of fluid . . . " "You have to go to labor and delivery." "But could it be...?" "You have to go get checked out now."

There was an urgency in her voice that bothered me, annoyed me. She didn't even let me explain the color or that it had been happening in small amounts or that I wasn't having any contractions. She didn't let me explain anything really. She heard the "f-word" and cut me off. I rolled my eyes and told Dan we had to go to the hospital. "They're going to send us home but I guess 'better safe than sorry.' They probably *have* to tell you to go in when they hear the word fluid. Some sort of liability thing, I bet." So we shrugged our shoulders, finished cleaning up dinner, and gathered our things. I already had my bag packed, so we grabbed the car seat just in case, and made our way down the road.

* * * * *

We checked in at the hospital at 8:00pm and the woman at the desk asked, "Are you ready to have your baby today?" "I doubt that I will but sure, why not?" I told her. I was still in complete denial. I wasn't experiencing the usual signs, the regular contractions, the rush of fluid. That's what was supposed to happen. There were two things that I did not want with this birth:

1. To be induced

2. To have a C-section

   I think you know where this is headed.

The nurse that helped us in triage was a doll. I wish that she had stayed with us through the labor and birth. She also asked if I was ready to have the baby, and again, like I was in some sort of denial fog, I said, "Sure, but I doubt that's happening." I mean, I wasn't in labor. I wasn't in pain. It wasn't like the movies or like the pregnancy books said or stories I'd heard from friends. So how could I possibly be about to have a baby?

A medical student came in and introduced herself. She asked if I would be ok with her helping out the doctor while they ran some tests to figure out if my water had broken. Sure. Why not? It felt full circle to have a medical student assisting my child's birth, since my own birth had been observed by medical students. The doctor on-call came in and she was also lovely and nice. She explained that there were several tests they had to conduct. She would check visually, do an ultrasound, and insert a speculum to see if there was any pooling of liquid. If there was, they would determine if it was amniotic fluid.

When she checked visually, she didn't notice anything of concern. In the end, when I had time to reflect, this made me feel less stupid about not going to the hospital sooner. I mean, I could only check visually . . . everything *seemed* normal. Then she did the speculum test and sure enough, there was pooling; meaning, a collection of liquid came out when the speculum opened up my vagina. This didn't necessarily mean my water had broken. They still had to test the liquid, which they did while they checked my water levels via ultrasound. Hmm . . . my water levels were at a 5. Two days before at my 40-week check-up the levels were at a 12. In fact, it was difficult for her to find water at all. She finally found a little pocket of water on the upper left of my uterus. And then the results were in on the liquid: amniotic fluid.

My water had broken.

And I had no idea.

Was I ready to have this baby? I guess I *had* to be ready.

I felt like a moron for not being able to realize what had been happening all day. My vision for how I wanted to labor was already wrong.

Then the next hammer to my heart: It was in my best interest, and the baby's, to be induced. Since I wasn't in active labor, but my water had broken, we were at risk for infection the longer we waited for my body to catch up. I could choose to wait, but the likelihood of complications would increase. I was *not* interested in being induced. I wanted to be bouncing on my exercise ball at home. The doctor said she'd give me some time to think about it and come back in a bit.

Here was my problem with inducing: from what I had heard, it was nearly impossible to avoid an epidural with Pitocin in play. The contractions would be too strong, too fast, and too unbearable. My fear was that once I got the epidural, things would slow down and the likelihood for a c-section would increase. I did NOT want a c-section. I hadn't even considered it as a possibility. That wasn't part of my birth story (or my birth fantasy as I've come to think of it). I wanted to see my baby boy enter the world. I wanted to hold him right away. I wanted to avoid drugs. My world was spinning and I was still only in the triage section of the maternity ward.

Our sweet nurse was very understanding about my hesitation, and she very calmly persuaded me that being induced would be best. I could try to go without drugs for as long as I wanted. No one would try to force me to do anything I didn't want to do, including having a c-section. So Dan and I decided, okay. Bring it on. Let's have our baby. Maybe even tonight! (insert laughter here)

* * * * *

The doctor and med student brought the nurse who would take care of me through the night. I don't remember her name. I do remember that she looked like a rounder-faced Anna Kendrick with too much eyeliner. She even kind of talked like her. I didn't find any of this comforting.

Turns out, this nurse was only at our hospital once a week. The upside of this was that she had a favorite room she liked to use when she was working and since it was available, she snagged it. And it *was* a nice room. The whole wall had windows looking out to the Hollywood Hills, where we watched the sun rise. I just didn't anticipate that we'd also get to see the sun set . . . but we'll get to that

part of the story soon enough.

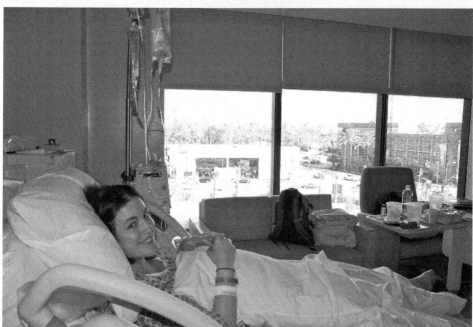

My Anna Kendrick nurse may have snagged me a great room, but that's about where her attributes fell off. Since she was only there once a week, she couldn't seem to remember where anything was or how the computer system worked. And when you're in the middle of full-blown labor, those extra few seconds spent fumbling around looking for the birthing ball or where to input information in your chart are *excruciating*. Even more so as the night wore on.

Around 10pm they started me on Pitocin: I was only a centimeter dilated. One fun fact: since you and your baby are at greater risk for infection once your water breaks, the medical staff limits the amount of internal exams they perform from there on. If you're curious about how dilated you are, it doesn't matter. Say you want to wait until you're about 4 or 5 centimeters dilated to receive an epidural because you've been told that if you wait until that point, the chances of needing a c-section will decrease. Too bad. They won't check more than once, maybe twice, during your induced labor.

Another fun fact: when you start on the Pitocin drip, contractions come on immediately. And they are intense. Unbearable. But regardless of the pain, I wanted to wait as long as I could to get an epidural because I was hell bent on avoiding a c-section. But I had no idea how much my dilation had progressed because they couldn't check me! It was a vicious battle between will and pain.

My Anna Kendrick nurse also reminded me of the six-fingered man from *The Princess Bride*. Remember when Wesley is tortured in the Pit of Despair and the six-fingered man slowly increases the voltage to shock him? And he keeps going higher because Wesley can tolerate more than he expects? Yep. That was my nurse. She'd say, "Hmm. You're handling this level of Pitocin pretty well. I think I'll increase it to a four." There was no emotion in her voice, but a slight glimmer in her eyes like she was enjoying the experiment. And then the next contraction would hit like a freight train.

* * * * *

I'm one of those people that actually prefers running on a treadmill because of the clock. I can see how long I've been running and I can see how much farther I have until I reach my goal. That's how I felt about labor. For example, if I knew I was at 3 centimeters, I thought I could tough it out until 4. But I didn't know how far dilated I was. Maybe if I did I could have held on longer. I don't know. All I know is that around 3:30AM, I was puking from the pain. Yes, I saw my steak again. And that's when I screamed, "GET ME THE EPIDURAL! I DON'T CARE WHAT I SAID BEFORE! I NEED IT NOW!" Just kidding. I wasn't that coherent. I think I nodded my consent with tears streaming down my face between retching.

When the epidural kicked in, I realized it was the best decision I had made through my entire labor. I laugh now when I think about going without it. After the epidural took effect, I tried to rest but that was difficult. Around 6AM the nurse finally decided it would be okay to do an internal exam to see how far I was dilated. I was at a 6. She said that was good. That meant I was probably at a 4 or 5 when I got my epidural, just like I had hoped. This made me feel better.

With the drugs keeping me calm and my dilation progressing nicely, I started to get a little excited. The sun was rising over the Hollywood Hills and it finally sunk in: I was going to meet my son today. Within a matter of hours, he'd be here. This was his birthday. I even posed for a picture:

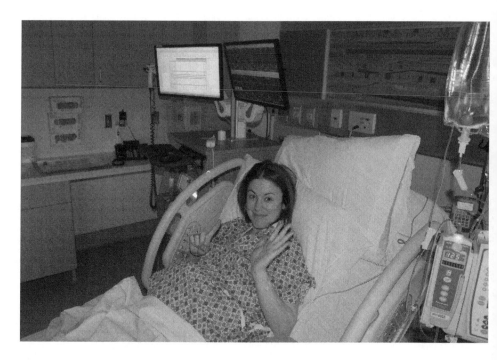

Six centimeters! A few hours later:

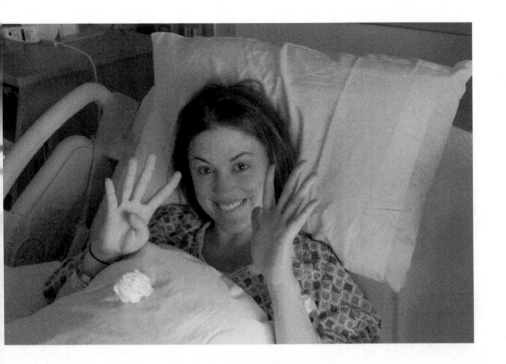

Nine centimeters!

By this time, Nurse Six-Fingered-Goth-Anna-Kendrick was gone and we had a jolly new nurse. She wore a bit too much perfume for my nauseated state, but she was warmer and kinder. I wish I could remember her name. Anyway, the especially good news was that it was Saturday and my doctor was the one on-call for the weekend. She works as part of a group so it wasn't guaranteed that she'd be my delivering doctor. This news was very reassuring. She knew how fervently I wanted to avoid a c-section and I knew she would be supportive. She would come in and check on me every now and then, and then more often as we got closer to full dilation. She told me she wanted me to wait to push until the baby was low enough that I would only be pushing for about an hour. Sounded good to me!

At noon she asked if I was ready to start pushing.

The time had come.

I was finally ready.

* * * * *

I've paused while writing the next part of this story. I'm not entirely sure how to best communicate it. Mostly because while I can give you a sequential narrative up until this point, I can't really do that with the telling of the next eight hours. I remember very distinct parts. But I don't remember always the order of those parts. It all kind of runs together. What follows is a hazy recollection (because of drugs, pain, stress), in as close to sequential order as I can piece together.

I started pushing. We waited for a contraction to start and then pushed three times, for a total of ten seconds on each push. They literally said, "Push like you're having a bowel movement!" So it's no wonder that most women (including myself) have just that. Which I only mention because I know so many of us are worried about it happening: Stop worrying. It will. In fact, the phrase "Shit Happens" probably came from childbirth.

At some point after I started pushing, I began to feel a dull pain in my lower back like a menstrual cramp was starting, which I mentioned to my doctor. It had been over ten hours since the epidural was administered and she thought it sounded like it was starting to wear off. She paged the anesthesiologist to come and give me another dose. In the approximately ten minutes it took for the anesthesiologist to arrive, I went from dull pain to OHMYGODMYINSIDESAREGOINGTORIPOUTOFMYBODY writhing pain. The Pitocin drip was still going and we made a new discovery: my baby was sunny-side-up. I'm having back labor as a result, which many women say is the worst kind of labor. The agony is exacerbated because a baby's head is not designed to come out of a body when he's facing up. I couldn't function. I couldn't push. I couldn't remember my name. It was definitely the worst pain I have ever experienced.

Aside from my doctor, I remember ONE person's name from the myriad of staff that helped bring Owen into the world. Her name is Alex. She was my anesthesiologist, and she became my angel. She and I got to know each other well over the next seven hours. She was no nonsense, yet still warm. She reminded me of the workout guru Jillian Michaels, of Biggest Loser fame. She seemed to truly care that I was having such a tough time, and she had this way of talking me down that made me feel like it was all going to be OK. She made a cocktail of meds and left it in the room in case another doc had to administer them. That was important later on. The first time my epidural wore off was the worst, but it happened several more times.

Three hours after beginning to push, Owen's head made its debut but just the very top; he was stuck. Another doctor came in. They wanted me to try pushing on all fours to try to get Owen to turn the right way. Have you ever had a limb fall asleep and then try to move it? NOT EASY. My legs were completely numb because Owen was lying on some sort of nerve. Somehow, with the help of Dan, my doctor, my nurse, and this new doctor, we got me turned over and someone propped my knees under me. Using only upper body strength to move all of my lower weight to stay in position while pushing was probably the toughest part of my labor. Like an animal I pushed on all fours, all of my bloated, naked, pregnant body exposed. Modesty? Every shred of it was gone.

At 7:00PM, after pushing on and off for seven hours, being awake for thirty-seven hours (when my water broke), having not eaten in nearly twenty-four hours (and having thrown up over seventeen hours earlier), being in active labor for nearly twenty-four hours, and pushing on all fours, the little sliver of Owen's head was still all that had made it's way out. I had to finally call it. I was not going to have my baby the way I had envisioned. I was beyond exhausted. I had done all that I could. My doctor told me earlier that I needed to consider either using a vacuum, which she did not believe would be very effective and could possibly cause damage to Owen, or having a c-section. Decision time.

Dan and I were both worn out. We were all each other had. We shook our heads and said, with hearts heavy from exhaustion and fear that we would go for the c-section.

As soon as the decision was made, things started moving very quickly. Doctors, nurses, people I'd never seen, started scurrying about. They were prepping the operating room, handing me paperwork to sign, telling Dan to pack up his stuff. It felt chaotic. I was so physically exhausted that I couldn't hold the pen to sign the paperwork. Dan was being told to do ten different things by ten different people and all he wanted to do was be by my side. But they wouldn't let him. I had to be prepped for surgery before he could come into the operating room. Suddenly we were both completely alone. Him more than me. I still had the sea of physicians prepping me. But this wasn't that comforting, especially because someone kept shouting, "Do you have the hemorrhage kit?" You can imagine this was a bit unnerving.

Once we were in the room, my angel Alex was back on the scene. If she wasn't there I'm not sure how I would've done. I was a mess. I couldn't stop shaking. I have no idea if it was from the freezing cold room, the epidural, the hormones, or my nerves, but I was literally rattling the metal table as I shook. And I was having a muscle spasm in my neck from all the pushing. I was crying, I was in pain, I couldn't lay my head down from the spasm, I was scared to death, and Dan wasn't there yet. Alex kept checking in with me, kept telling me that as soon as Owen was born she was going to give me medicine for the muscle spasm and for the shaking. She reassured me that everything was going to be ok. She told me to think ahead, to imagine the wine and the sushi and all of the yummy stuff I could finally have again as soon as he was born. I didn't have the heart to tell her that I was the one person in California who didn't eat sushi. I just kept trying to breathe through my hysteria.

After what seemed like an eternity, Dan was finally allowed into the room. He was just as shell-shocked as me. He told me later that he called his parents while he waited in the hallway and cried.

He was so scared that we might not make it. And there wasn't anyone there to hold his hand and let him know that it was going to be ok. And when he finally did get to see me, he found me worse— shaking violently, crying, in worse pain. Things weren't looking good.

But ready or not, Owen was coming.

At 7:57 PM, nearly eight hours after we started pushing and nearly twenty-four hours since we'd gotten to the hospital, Owen was finally, *finally,* born.

* * * * *

I don't remember hearing him cry for the first time. I didn't see him for nearly ten minutes after he was born; my neck hurt so badly I couldn't turn to look at him. But the drug cocktail Alex made was starting to work, and the shaking was starting to lessen. And then one of the doctors held him up for me to see. My baby boy. I felt such a strange combination of emotions: relief, grief, happiness, pride, exhaustion. He was here. And all I wanted to do was fall

asleep.

Eyes-wide-open-Owen

Owen had done great. My doc said, "He was staring right at me, eyes wide open, just waiting, when I took him out." Alert from the moment he entered the world. The back of his head had been rubbed raw from where he had been stuck in my pelvis, trying to get out, just as determined as his mama. He had a scab there for the first three weeks of his life. We had battled together long and hard and had the scars to prove it.

I *always* expected to feel a tidal wave of love, unlike anything I had ever experienced, when I saw my baby for the first time. Instead, I felt almost numb. This wasn't how it was supposed to be. And my lack of emotion scared me.

With the gift of hindsight, I realize that this story could have been much worse. I've talked with friends and read stories of women since who had a much scarier time giving birth. Cords wrapped around necks, hearts stopping, hemorrhaging, all of it. A month after giving birth I was relaying my story to a friend and she casually remarked, "It's crazy though. A hundred years ago, you would both be dead." And I gained a little appreciation. Things may have not

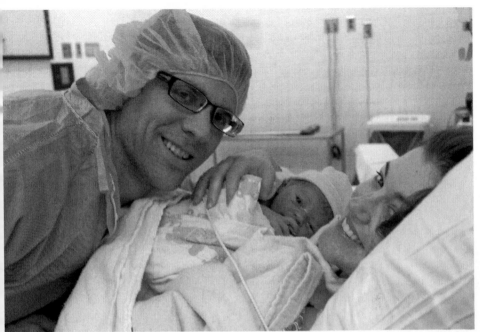
First family photo.

happened the way I was hoping but we are both here. And as the
cliché goes, that is what matters most. Another friend who gave birth
a few weeks before me had also wanted to have as natural a birth as
possible but ended up with an emergency c-section. She said
something that really stuck with me: Her maternity yoga instructor
had reminded her mamas during their practice that when it comes
down to it, your baby's birthday is *their birthday. Not ours.* That they
are coming into the world exactly as they are supposed to. As first-
time-moms we have in our head visions of how things are
"supposed" to go when we give birth. We take classes, read books,

envision outcomes and even though we say we're ready "for anything," for me, that wasn't true.

I had lost perspective and it took me awhile to get it back.

Chapter 5

First Day Home

After sobbing from the moment I left the hospital room, I shuffled into our apartment and collapsed. The tears continued. Dan unloaded the car and Owen sat in his car seat in the middle of the living room. I was on my knees, holding onto the rug for support, heaving. Grieving. I wasn't supposed to be home with a baby. He wasn't supposed to be here yet. Not like this. It was Tuesday. When I left Friday night I didn't think that the next time I'd see our home, Owen would be out of my body, let alone in a car seat, hungry and tired, sitting on our living room floor. The whole first few days at home felt like a trance.

Now when I look back, I can see myself so clearly. I'm raw and broken. My body hurts in ways I can't comprehend. My muscles ache in my back, in my neck, in my belly, in my heart, from pushing for seven hours. My caesarean incision throbs; it's tender to the slightest brush of fabric. I take all the underwear I bought for postpartum recovery and cut off the elastic band in the front, so it won't irritate my stitches. After climbing the stairs, clinging to the railing, pausing at each step, I lay down on our bed. My insides feel like they are sliding out of the gaping wound in my belly. I panic. I can't lay down. My body will burst open and I'll slowly die as my uterus and intestines and bladder and all my vital organs seep out of my body. My abdominal muscles are so weak, I can't use them to stand back up. I have to edge myself off the side of the bed so that I can use my arms to stand. Everything is wrong. I haven't slept since Thursday night. There have been snippets of dozing, but I haven't gotten any decent rest in five days. I've also undergone a physical trauma and now have to sustain a tiny human with breast milk that hasn't come in yet. All of my energy is being sucked out of me as my body tries to heal and my baby tries to survive.

Since I can't lay in the bed, Dan moves the rocker/recliner upstairs to our bedroom so I have a place to rest. It breaks down into two pieces, which makes it only slightly easier to carry solo. But he's powering off adrenaline and is able to he-man his way through to get me settled and comfortable. He assembles the rocker next to his side of the bed because there is more room. Plus it's next to the window so at least I can have a bit of a view while I convalesce. I don't think I ever opened the blinds more than a crack during my confinement in that chair. He sets up a baby station. The little pink tub we got at the hospital is full of gauze and petroleum jelly to dress Owen's circumcision wound. Diapers and gauze to clean him after he poops and pees. No wipes yet. He's still too sensitive and new, and his skin is too easily irritated. There are blankets to swaddle him, but we soon realize that the blankets we have are too long, too gossamer-thin to swaddle. We made the mistake of not taking any blankets from the hospital. Those blankets were sturdier, a better size for swaddling. Those are the blankets Dan used to learn how to swaddle. Owen won't lay down without being swaddled. He screams and breaks free from all of our attempts to wrap him. We get out swaddling instructions for these particular blankets. Still can't figure it out. YouTube videos don't help. Didn't someone give us one of those zip-up-swaddle-things? Can't find it. And when we do, they are still too big for his little seven-pounds-and-losing-weight body. I tell Dan to go back to the hospital and tell them we need some blankets. I tell him I'll hold Owen until he gets back. That's what I say, but what I'm thinking is, "Please don't leave. Please don't leave me alone. Please don't leave me alone with him." But I don't see another solution. Thankfully, Dan doesn't go. He probably senses my panic, knows that he shouldn't leave. He keeps trying to get the swaddle to work with the blankets that we have. And, like a small miracle, he does. I never am able to swaddle as well as him.

Not only is my swaddling deficient, I can't get up if Owen cries. I can't help change diapers. I can't pick him up out of the pack and play if he needs to be fed. Not that he will let us put him down for any extended period of time. I can't get up out of the chair if I'm holding him. I can't feed him. Every time I try, he latches on for a minute and then starts screaming. I manipulate my breast, squeeze and reposition. I try every angle to make it easier for him to eat. Nothing works. I hook myself up to the pump we rented from the hospital and eke out a few ounces. It's nothing thick and white and creamy like I expect at this point. It's just thin and yellowish and syrupy and I'm pretty sure my child is going to starve to death because I can't produce milk. We already had to start supplementing with formula at the hospital, but I don't want to have to give him formula because "breast is best," right? So I pump and try to get him to latch. But we have to start an alternating feeding schedule with breast milk and formula. I've already failed. Again.

I'm still unable to stop crying. Every time Owen finally falls asleep I try to rest, but I have to set an alarm and wake him every three hours to eat. Then, after he eats, I have to pump for twenty minutes. Every time I try to fall asleep, I feel panicked. I feel jittery and unable to shut my eyes.

I'm not going to make it.

Dan takes care of everything. Owen and me and maybe himself, but I'm not entirely sure about that last one. He's making me food, he's changing diapers, he's keeping track of wet diapers and poop diapers and the color of all the bodily waste. He's putting that info into a spreadsheet so we can track it and make sure Owen is getting enough to eat. He's swaddling and dressing and making sure my cup is full of water and holding and helping and resting when all is quiet. He's slept about as much as me and we're in a fragile, desperate state.

Chapter 6

The Calls We Made on Wednesday

The sun finally rises on Wednesday and I'm certain I'm not going to be okay if I don't sleep. Or eat. Or have my mom with me. She's scheduled to fly in on Saturday, but I'm positive I'm not going to see Saturday if we don't get help. And not just any help. I need my mom.

First we call my ob/gyn.

I cry and tell her that I'm not ok. She asks if I've slept. I tell her I can't. Every time I try to sleep, I panic. She is emphatic that I need to rest and prescribes me Ambien. She says to take it as soon as possible. It'll help me sleep for eight hours. Eight hours?? Eight hours sounds completely unreasonable to me. I can't sleep for that long. I have to feed Owen. I have to pump. I have to be there to help Dan. Even though I haven't been able to help up to this point, in my manic state I'm certain that I have to at least be awake and try to help. She calls in a prescription to my pharmacy despite my less than enthusiastic response.

I call my mom. "Mom. I'm not ok. Please. I don't care what you have to do. I don't care what it costs. I'll pay it. But can you please get on the next flight here? I'm not ok." The answer is, of course, yes. And it's only now that I'm healthy and a few years into being a mother that I realize how frightening that call must have been for her. If she could have jumped on a plane the second we got off the phone, I'm certain she would have done it.

I know a little more now, now that a few years have passed. There is a tone in Owen's voice that is unmistakable when he is scared. A tremor in the way he shouts, "Mommy!" I hear it when he has fallen out of his "big-boy-bed" in the middle of the night. Even though his bed is against the wall and has a toddler rail on the other side, he still manages to roll off from the foot of the bed from time to time. I hear his scared shout of my name through the baby monitor and it doesn't matter how deeply I'm sleeping, adrenaline takes over, and I'm up and in his room within seconds. I get down on the floor and he crawls into my lap, nestled as close as he can, crying as he tries to catch his breath from the shock of the fall. I ask him where it hurts and he tells me — his bottom, his back, his arm. Sometimes it doesn't hurt anywhere. He's just had the wind knocked out of him. I try to soothe him with rocking and snuggles and reassurances until he can rest again.

I imagine that the maternal instinct to comfort and reassure will never go away, whether Owen is three or thirty. So when my mom heard the fear in my voice, from three time zones away, it couldn't have been easy. She says she will call me back as soon as she knows when she can get here.

I talk to Dan about the Ambien. I tell him I don't want to be asleep for that long. I don't want to not be able to help. And he says in the most gracious and loving way, "You have to take it. You have to sleep. You're no good to us if you don't. *We'll be fine.*" And he means it. He's scared and unsure, but he doesn't let on. He convinces me. Now the next complication. How on earth are we going to be able to get this medication from the pharmacy? And that's when I get a text from my friend Corinne.

"Hey! Thinking of you. Let me know if you need anything!"

It's Wednesday morning and I know she doesn't work on Wednesdays because that's when we normally go hiking together. And she does only live ten minutes away, and said, "if I need anything." I know she means it.

And this is how Corinne becomes the first person to meet our son.

I call and murmur through my crying, "If it's in any way possible, could you do a Target run for us? I have a prescription I need and there's this rocker/bassinet thing I saw that I think might be the only way Owen will sleep and we need more formula and maybe you can just stop by first and I can give you a small list? Please?" She arrives within thirty minutes.

I've told her since and I'll say it again: I am forever indebted to her for coming over and helping that day. She insists that it was "no big deal" but it was *everything* in that moment. She came in, she didn't judge, she didn't cringe at how badly the room surely smelled or how broken I surely looked, covered in various bodily fluids from both the baby and me. She listened empathetically as I cried and confessed how hard it was. How the birth went. How I couldn't sleep. How Owen wouldn't sleep unless he was held. How I was a failure at breastfeeding. How I was in so much pain. I was completely vulnerable and she held my hand and I felt understood. Finally having the opportunity to talk about everything that had happened since Friday night felt like such an unburdening. The hour she sat with me before heading to the store was as beneficial, if not more so, than the sleep I so desperately needed.

A few weeks later I learned that her mom is a nurse and used to take Corinne with her on house calls to check on new mothers. Unbeknownst to me, the friend that reached out and who I clung to like a life preserver after a shipwreck, is the one who was the best equipped to help me in those early days. She had seen the gamut of new-mom states and insists that I was certainly not the worst she'd encountered.

We'd been friends for about five years at that point. We met through mutual friends, starred in a web series together, and become part of each other's inner circle. We went on weekly hikes, all the way until my seventh month of pregnancy. And somehow her new-motherhood-know-how never came up. I still think it's crazy. But my mom would likely say, "Not really," with a knowing smile. She has always insisted that I have a guardian angel watching out for me, and that coincidences like that are not coincidences at all. She may be right. On that Wednesday, Corinne was my angel.

And speaking of my mom, she had found a flight that landed at 9:30am the next morning. There was suddenly an endpoint to look toward. Just like running on a treadmill. I could track the hours until she arrived. Knowing that there was a tangible finish line made life seem livable.

Chapter 7

help.

Thursday morning was a new beginning. I took the sleeping pill on Wednesday to try to gain a little equilibrium. It was supposed to knock me out for eight hours. After four hours I was wide-awake and the house was quiet. I managed to get out of my recliner and shuffle over to the nursery, where I knew I'd find Dan and Owen. Dan was sitting on the floor, propped against the daybed, holding Owen while both of them slept. He was worried that he'd drop Owen if he fell asleep so he had surrounded himself with pillows. He looked up groggily and asked what I was doing up.

"I'm just checking on you guys."

"We're fine. Go back to sleep."

I shuffled back to my recliner in my drugged state.

I was rested enough in the morning to make my way downstairs and watch for my mom's arrival through the kitchen window. I remember a white cab pulling up and her dark hair blowing in the wind as she waited for the driver to pull her luggage out of the trunk. I couldn't wait any longer so I unlocked the front door and stood in the doorway while she paid.

She stepped onto our porch and a sense of home and balance washed over me as we hugged.

"Hi Mama," I said through tears. "I'm so glad you're here."

I was so relieved to have my mom there. I have a framed picture of her holding Owen for the first time shortly after her arrival. It's in a four-frame set. The first picture is of her, super pregnant with me. The next picture is my grandma, her mom, holding me as an infant. The third picture is of me super pregnant with Owen and the final picture is of her holding Owen for the first time. It's one of my most treasured possessions. I come from a line of wonderful, strong mothers. Their examples have shown me how to be a loving parent. These pictures remind me that I'm carrying on what they started—that I can be a great mother too. Which is not how I felt those first days home.

I've always been close to my mom. When I was growing up, I never understood when my friends got embarrassed by their moms or didn't want them around. I *wanted* my mom around. She was a friend, the first person I wanted to tell my news, happy or sad. I wanted her opinion when I went through difficult times and I wanted her ear to just vent if I needed. I was newly 21 when I moved to NYC. I called her everyday and we'd talk about everything and nothing. And now that there's FaceTime? Forget about it. We talk at least three times a week, while we eat breakfast, before she heads out to work. It's amazing; she gets to watch Owen grow and play. One of my great regrets is that I didn't think that it was imperative to have my mom at the hospital when Owen was born. It was admittedly tricky to figure out the travel details and her work schedule since we didn't know when he'd arrive. But when his due date came and went, I should have said, "Mom, why don't you just come out and hopefully he'll be here soon?" I'm sure we could have made it work. But I didn't. And I didn't realize how comforting it would be to have her near. She'd always been my touchstone, which is why I knew it would make all the difference once she got there.

But then, it didn't exactly.

* * * * *

Flash forward eight months:

Standing in line, waiting to check in for our "mommy and me" yoga class. Another mother with a son about a month younger than Owen was waiting with me. We'd been in class together for a few months at this point so there was a casual camaraderie established; we'd chitchat. In front of us, there was a new mom checking into the class. New to the class, new to motherhood. Her baby was all of eight weeks old, fresh and new and just now getting exposed to the world. And my friend sighs, "Wow, I miss that time." I looked at her nearly cross-eyed, "You do?" "Yeah, it was so magical," she replied wistfully. And I responded truthfully, "Wow, not for me." And then I was quick to qualify, "I mean, Owen was

great. I just. Wasn't." And then it was time to swipe my key tag and

pay for parking and the conversation was over and she didn't ask

any questions and we both continued to juggle our babies from hip

to hip as we reached for our money and struggled to keep our diaper

bags and yoga bags from falling off our shoulders. And then we were

off to class and that was that. It was the first time I admitted aloud,

to a relative stranger, that all was not roses and candy for me as a

mother. And it was strange to do so because she clearly had a very

different experience than me. She sounded more like my mother.

My mom doesn't remember those first days of motherhood as

being hard. She doesn't seem to remember them much at all. Fair

enough. She's been a mom now for over thirty years. That was a long

time ago. But it seems to me, in my limited experience, that those

who have a terrible time in the beginning don't forget how bad it

was, no matter how much time has passed. And yes, it is a common

coping mechanism to block out the bad so it's entirely possible that

my mom had a tougher time than she allows herself to remember.

But. *She doesn't remember*. So when I was in those new, raw days and the only other mother I had to talk to and relate to was my own mother, I felt even more alone.

* * * * *

I had my first breakdown the day after she arrived. That first day I was too high on having her near, not on a phone, but as a tangible part of my day. The next day those euphoric feelings couldn't combat the despair any longer. Owen was finally asleep, it was the middle of the day, and I gingerly made it down the stairs, clinging to the railing. My mom was sitting on the couch and I sat down carefully next to her. It was quiet for a moment. Then I started crying. And crying. I couldn't stop. I was near hysteria. I told her that I had made a mistake. I couldn't be a mom. I regretted ever wanting to be one. And through my tears I saw her face. And what I saw was fear. Fear that I interpreted as *she doesn't know how to help me*. My mom, who always seemed to know what to do or what to say or how to listen, seemed to be at a loss. She didn't seem to understand or know how to direct me. It was scary, for her and for me. My mom who had a "textbook birth" with me, a quick delivery with my brother, and an uneventful one with my sister. My mom who doesn't remember much from when we were infants, but from what she does remember, there weren't any of the vast lows I was experiencing. She doesn't remember despair or regret or crippling anxiety. All of this is new for her. All of this is unexpected for both of us.

She couldn't relate because she had a very different birth experience with all three of her children. She told me as much. And she told me I just needed to get some sleep. Things would look better if I could just rest.

There's no doubt, looking back, that she was right. Your body and your brain cannot heal properly if you don't have access to restorative rest in order to rebuild. But hearing "you just need to rest" at that moment, after having taken Ambien, and now feeling like sleep *wasn't* the solution because I *had* slept and I still felt this abyss of pain, wrecked me. My mom's words of comfort and reassurance fell on deaf ears. It was not what I wanted to hear. I'm not sure what the right answer would have been. But I think maybe I wanted to hear that I wasn't alone. That other mothers feel like this in those tender days immediately after giving birth. That I wasn't crazy for feeling crazy. That it would get better because I would get better.

And that's, I think, when I started to shutdown. I certainly don't blame my mom for my shutdown. But I suddenly felt like the partner I'd had all my life, didn't understand what I was going through. I didn't know where else to turn. And my urge to protect *her* took over. I didn't want to see that look of fear and helplessness again. I wanted at least one thing in my life to be like it was before I fell down this rabbit hole. So I just stopped talking about how I was feeling. I'd swallow it up, I'd cry when I was alone, I'd force myself to be my old self. While I certainly couldn't hide my fragility those three weeks she stayed with us, I just didn't talk about it. And it was easier to mask once she was home and I was alone again.

Chapter 8

Marcia's Note

A note from my mama, in her own words:

Meagan,

From the time you were just a little girl, you have had a vision about what your future would hold. You would become an actress, wife, and mother. Also along the way you would make a difference in this world by touching the lives of many as a best friend and/or mentor, or maybe with just a smile or kind words to brighten someone's day. These dreams have all become realities. What you didn't anticipate was that the journey might not go exactly as planned, especially the motherhood part.

Your entire pregnancy was picture perfect so of course you would expect the delivery to be smooth sailing as well. I had no doubt that you would have a textbook delivery, just as I did when you were born. Therefore, I decided that the best time for me to arrive in LA from Florida would be after Owen was born and you were back home and my assistance would be more beneficial. In hindsight, I really wish I had jumped on a plane the minute you were admitted to the hospital, but because of my job it was hard to plan it out that way.

When you called me crying hysterically the day after you got home begging me to come right away, I immediately booked a flight and got there as soon as I could. You kept saying you and Dan had not gotten any sleep for at least 24 hours. I think at the time you were blaming your feelings on sleep deprivation, hormones, your unplanned c-section along with many other possible explanations. These excuses all seemed logical to me. I thought as soon as you got a good night's sleep and your body healed, you would be good as new. You have always been so natural and maternal with children, I never thought otherwise.

I have not had much experience in dealing with depression, so I have to admit that in your case, I failed to recognize the signs. Being a new mother can be quite exhausting so when you didn't seem your normal upbeat, cheery self that actually seemed normal under the circumstances. There was nothing in your actions that indicated, at least to me, that something was seriously wrong. I definitely did not know how bad the depression had gotten. Did you hide it that well or did I just miss it that bad?

The reality is, things on the inside are not always as they appear on the outside. Hopefully, by telling your story you will inspire others to get the help they need and deserve and to realize they are not alone.

I love you!

Chapter 9

One Week Old

He'd been in the world exactly a week. The hospital sent us

home with a printout of ways to care for him and what to look out

for. What should concern you and what shouldn't. How many times a

day he should pee and poop. How much he should eat. What his

temperature should be. Personality changes to watch for. Warning

signs that could mean your brand-new child might not be thriving.

Dan created two spreadsheets for tracking Owen: one for his

bathroom habits and one for how much he was eating. Since I had to

pump and supplement, we had a pretty good idea of how many

ounces he was taking in. And if he did nurse, we recorded how many

minutes, and on which breast. Looking back, we were probably a little too meticulous. Am I understating the obvious? Probably. But when everything else feels out of control, sometimes making a spreadsheet of the things you *can* control brings a sense of peace. And in our case, we could control our observations of the input and output of this little human being.

On Day 6, something shifted. In days prior, I was setting an alarm for every three hours so that I could wake him up to feed. He much preferred to sleep than eat, but usually he'd eat when awakened. But on Day 6, he started to fall asleep as he was eating. And he felt cool to the touch. And he was lethargic. I mean, newborns are lethargic. It's their general nature. But he couldn't seem to stay awake. I was already certain he wasn't getting enough to eat because I couldn't produce milk, but now it seemed like it was catching up with him. We took his temperature rectally, as instructed in our printout, and it was lower than the printout said was normal. In fact, the printout said to immediately seek help if it was lower than a certain degree.

We promptly freaked the eff out.

We called our pediatrician's office and the on-call doctor —
Dr. Poopyhead (real name changed to protect the idiotic) — was the
one to take our questions. He sounded bored as I told him about how
Owen was acting and what his temperature was and what the
printout said. He said not to worry because the temperature was not
really a big concern. The printout was just a guideline; he wasn't
concerned. This did not soothe me. I remembered Dr. Poopyhead
from our stay at the hospital. He was the pediatrician on-call the day
we were discharged. He strolled into our hospital room in jeans and
a Hawaiian shirt, stethoscope around his neck. No white coat. He
was too laid back and "cool" on that day, too. We were concerned
because Owen's billirubin test was inconclusive and we weren't sure
if he had jaundice or not. And the nurse told us to make sure to bring
that up with the pediatrician that checked Owen out. So we did, and
he scoffed and dismissed our concerns. "Nurses overreact," was his
response. Well, sir, I happen to believe that nurses are literally the
backbone of the medical profession. I don't think of them as
superfluous or over-reactive. So already I don't trust you. And your

Johnny B. Cool demeanor with your jeans and no coat is not doing you any favors to win my trust.

So here I was, at home, on a 6am call with Dr. Poopyhead who said, "I think he's fine BUT if you're really concerned, you can take him to urgent care. It doesn't open until 9am. And you risk exposing him to whatever people may have that are going there. But, you know, do what you want." No matter what he said, I wasn't going to believe him.

That's how we ended waiting up behind four sick people outside a closed urgent care on Owen's one-week birthday. My mom and I stood in line, and Dan waited in the car with Owen so that he wouldn't be exposed to all the sickies until we went in to see the doctor. I was wearing all black and leaning against the wall for support. I still wasn't completely steady on my feet.

When it was time to see the doctor, Dan carried Owen in the car seat with a blanket draped over to protect him from germs. The doctor was a kind and upbeat woman who immediately made me feel a little more at ease. She checked Owen out, took his temperature, and determined that he was fine. She said the printout was just a guideline and we didn't have to be concerned. Yes. I had heard this exact sentiment earlier from Dr. Poopyhead but didn't trust it until I heard it from her. With her personable nature and *white coat,* she was way more trustworthy.

And then she turned her attention to me.

"How are you doing, Mommy?"

I nearly crumbled. I wasn't expecting the question.

"Ok. Not great, I guess. He cries a lot when I try to feed him." She asked if I wouldn't mind trying to feed him now. I said ok. And, of course, he latched on right away. No screaming. Just eating. Who was this kid? She could have gone to her next patient right then and dismissed my concerns like I felt everyone else had so far, but she stayed. And asked how my milk production was. And I was like, "Ok. Not great, I guess." She recommended fenugreek and Mother's Milk Tea. She took her time telling me about places where I could get pure fenugreek seed to add to my food and drink. Then she asked, "What's your favorite meal?" I responded, unintentionally childlike, that I loved my mom's spaghetti. She turned her attention to my mom and said kindly, "Mom, you need to make her spaghetti." She said I needed to eat more and take care of myself, that my baby boy was just fine and would be even better if I, too, felt better. She told me she was a mother of three and was still breastfeeding her youngest. She was able to see my struggles in a way that I wasn't even fully aware of yet. And she connected to me as only those who have been there could.

Turns out I needed that trip to urgent care more than Owen did.

And I got a delicious spaghetti meal that night, with plenty of leftovers for the days following. Spaghetti is always yummier as a leftover.

Chapter 10

So This Is What Depression Looks Like

A few days later, when Owen was ten days old, my sister Kelsey arrived in town. Kelsey is a woman of many talents. She's a ridiculously gifted musician; she can play three instruments, write songs, sing like an angel; she even wrote a song as a surprise gift for Dan and me at our wedding. She paints. She is a bit of a prodigy in the advertising business, having worked for two of the largest ad agencies in the world all before the age of 25. She sees the world differently; her perspective is usually uplifting with a dash of humor. And all of these factors make her a really fantastic photographer. I knew I wanted her to take Owen's newborn photos. I had lots of ideas pinned on Pinterest for family shots, but when our photo shoot day rolled around I could barely walk and the idea of showering sounded like a long shot. Putting on makeup and doing my hair? Laughable. But somehow I rallied. "The show must go on" mantra is well-ingrained in this actress.

We started with shots of Owen in a sweet owl hat that one of his aunts had crocheted. Then there were the obligatory naked shots. We had him curled on the couch in a way that hid his parts, but you could still see his sweet new form. Yes, he peed on the couch. There were the close-ups of all of his little features — his long fingers and the curl of hair at the nape of his head.

And then it was time for the family shots. I feel tired just thinking about the session. Deep in my bones I can still feel the exhaustion I felt on that day. All I wanted to do was cry, but I had put on makeup so I was going to power through. I wasn't going to risk messing up my makeup with tears. Priorities, man.

We decided that Owen's nursery would be a good place to take most of our pictures. And it was. The light came in soft through the window, and the neutral gray-blue painted walls complemented the light. In the middle of the session, there was a moment when Dan was holding Owen in one arm and had his other arm wrapped around my shoulders. We quietly whispered to one another about how miserable we were. "I'm so tired." "Me too." "When are we going to be done?" "I don't know." My head is nestled into the crook of Dan's neck and I lean on him because I literally can't stand on my own. We were laughing quietly, slightly manically, at the absurdity of it all and I take a moment just to breathe . . . and . . . click.

Magic.

It's a beautiful picture.

When I look at it, I can tell that I'm about to cry. And I can tell that if you didn't know better — and honestly, how would you? —you'd probably interpret my expression as one of an overjoyed mother, enamored with the new life sweetly sleeping in his father's arms. At some point I decide to post it on Facebook as my cover photo, and almost instantly the likes and comments start pouring in. "Beautiful!" "Congrats!" "So perfect!" One guy I went to middle school with wrote, "So this is what happiness looks like! Congrats!" I let out a cynical guffaw when I read that one and had to read it aloud to Dan.

If he only knew. We've got them all fooled, folks! Life is just a bowl of cherries over here.

A picture is worth a thousand words. And in this case, the words were all lies.

But we looked the part—the part of the tired, yet grateful parents, soaking in the bliss of our new position in the world. We're presented with images through television and movies, and now through social media, of how new parenthood is supposed to look. There is *always* the deep sigh. When a new parent takes a moment to breathe in the new baby smell and revel in its sweetness. In my case, however, I took a deep sigh because I had to remind myself to *actually breathe*. The powdery, perfumed smell of Owen's diapers made me want to vomit so I had to breathe to keep the puke down. I also literally had to breathe through the pain of the surgery. I had to breathe through the sadness I felt was consuming me. And I had to breathe through my dark confusion. My emotions felt nothing like what I had expected or desired. The deep sigh immortalized in that photo was certainly worth a thousand words, but none that resembled sweetness, bliss, or contentment. I posted that photo because it *looked* pretty; it conveyed what I wanted the world to see. But that photo was a lie. I probably posted it even *more so* because I knew it was a lie. That picture made it seem like we were okay. That I was okay. That we were better than okay. That picture made us look like the pure essence of happiness.

Maybe if everyone thought I was happy, I'd start to feel like I was.

I wasn't just trying to create a narrative for everyone else, I was trying to create one for myself. I was fighting against the darkness that was taking over, trying to dig myself out of the hole that kept getting deeper.

Chapter 11

Breastfeeding. Or not.

When Owen was nine-weeks old, about two months after our urgent care trip, I finally gave up the charade. I wanted so badly to breastfeed. My plan was to breastfeed exclusively for the first six months before introducing foods and then continue to breastfeed to at least his first birthday. If he wanted or needed to nurse longer than that, I was open to the idea. "Breast is best" is a catchy little rhyme that really stuck with me. And those that believe that rhyme are passionate. And I'm a passionate person. And everyone wants what is best for her child. At nine weeks into his life, I realized what was best had nothing to do with rhymes.

There is an ugly thing going on in our mommy culture. There is too much information and too much access to each other's lives to not feel utterly bombarded by opinions. And opinions that masquerade as fact are the scariest of them all. When you are a new mom like I was, without a strong mama community to turn to in those early weeks, you start diving into virtual communities. And the loudest voices in those communities were pro-breastfeeding. Perhaps a better way to put it is anti-formula. I felt like if I gave my baby formula, I was depriving him of so many things. Vitamins, nutrients, antibodies, bonding time. If I couldn't give him the goods straight from the source, then I better pump so that he could at least get part of the equation. If I didn't, then I clearly don't care if he developed asthma down the line. If I gave him formula, then it would be my fault when his immune system didn't hold up against the common cold.

But I was not equipped to successfully breastfeed. In the hospital, the lactation nurses came to my room regularly. It would be time to feed Owen, and he'd wail when held to my breast. He wouldn't latch on with any sort of consistency. One nurse said it was because of the trauma of his birth. There was such tension in his mouth that he couldn't latch on. They insisted I use the industrial pump to help get my supply in. I needed to try to nurse him every three hours because his weight was on the steady decline and he was already less than eight pounds. After nursing—whether he had latched on or not—I was to hook up to the pump for twenty minutes on each side. We rented the machine and took it home with us for the first month. I continued that routine for those first four weeks: Nurse or bottle feed every three hours, and then pump for twenty minutes on each side. I was meticulous about it. I had eight alarms set through each 24-hour cycle. I watched as the clock on my phone "sprung forward" for daylight savings at 2am one night in March. It sprang right past an alarm I had set for 2:30am. Good thing I wasn't sleeping that night (or any night, really). Days didn't have a beginning and an end. I was living in three-hour intervals.

The entire time I used the hospital-grade pump, I never pumped more than four ounces on either breast. And four ounces felt like a real victory. Most of the time I averaged around 2 or 3 ounces. Once I returned the pump and started using my own, I couldn't even suction that much out.

I clearly wasn't producing much milk. I definitely wasn't producing enough. Supplementing had started in the hospital and continued pretty much every other feeding. Every feeding I would try to get him to latch on. And even when he did, I still made sure he had a bottle as well, whether it was pumped milk or formula. He always drank it.

I drank mother's tea and ate a lot of oats. I tried to eat and drink as much water as I could to get my supply up. I would drink water while I nursed to keep things flowing. I sat on the phone for over an hour with a La Leche League volunteer that first week after he was born. She gave me as many tips as she could, but at the end of the conversation she said, "He needs to eat. You have to give him formula." I'm pretty sure she could get excommunicated or whatever they do to breast traitors for that piece of advice. But it was the truth. I needed to do what was best for my baby.

It took ten days for my colostrum, the yellowish-thin, nutrient-rich liquid that is first secreted from the breast, to turn into milk. It usually takes three-to-five days for this transition. But I don't think my milk ever fully "came in." I never had enough.

I was never enough.

That's what my breastfeeding failure felt like. It magnified all of my deficiencies I'd felt since giving birth. The lack of connection. The lack of "natural ability." The lack of "true" love.

I was lacking.

One could argue that I didn't do enough. I should have gone to a center where they had lactation consultants. I should have called a nurse to come to my house. I should have continued pumping. I should have gotten the fenugreek seed that the amazing doctor at urgent care recommended. I should have kept going.

But at nine weeks postpartum, after pumping for twenty minutes and only getting one ounce of milk, I said no more.

I packed up my pump and stocked up on formula.

I changed my alarms from every three hours to every four.

Owen started sleeping longer at night. I stopped setting alarms. *I* started sleeping longer at night.

He gained weight.

I gained back a little sanity, or at least gained a little equilibrium.

Breastfeeding was not the best choice for my mental health. The non-sleep cycle with the non-production of milk was devastating for me in the early days. Dan begged me to stop. He argued that he was exclusively bottle fed as a baby and he turned out all right. He could see how hard I was trying and how far behind I was. I told him it was best for our baby and kept going like a stubborn mule. Or milk cow.

Once I finally stopped I realized something. What is best for my baby, what is best for any baby, is a healthy mother. A physically and mentally healthy mother. If breastfeeding is the easy part of new motherhood for a woman, then she should breastfeed. If it's not . . . THAT'S OK. And totally normal. Why else would there be professional lactation consultants? Or entire shopping aisles at the grocery store dedicated to all the different kinds of formula on the market? Sometimes breastfeeding simply isn't as "natural" as it seems it should be.

I wonder now whether my inability to produce milk had anything to do with my extended physical recovery from the exhausting labor and unexpected c-section. It feels like it has to be related. With my next child, I'm going to give breastfeeding another shot. I hope to have the feeding experience I longed for with Owen. But if it doesn't work out again? I'm not going to let myself spiral into self-shame and bottomless guilt like I did with Owen. I know now how detrimental that was for my mental and physical health. And I know that Owen is as healthy and strong as they come, and that he's gotten that way with a little bit of mother's milk and a whole lot of formula in his first year of life.

Chapter 12

Early Dismissal

I *expected* to feel a rollercoaster of emotions after delivery. The books tell you, your friends tell you, the doctors tell you: Your hormones are straight up cray cray after having a bay bay. "Baby Blues" (also, the name of a yummy BBQ joint in LA) is a common term tossed around so I fully expected to start crying for no reason or miss being pregnant or feel incredibly high with love only to come crashing down to Sadville in the next moment. I even had a Twitter exchange a few weeks before delivery with the writer/creator of my new favorite sitcom at the time. She is a friend of a friend and I knew that she worked throughout her pregnancy to create her first network show. I was astounded by her. I couldn't imagine being pregnant for the first time and producing a show at that level. So I sent her kudos via the great equalizing medium of social media. We went back and forth for a few 140-character tweets about her show and being a new mom. Then I mentioned how I was due soon and she sent back, ". . . .The first couple weeks are VERY HARD, but it gets easier and easier. And don't worry if you feel sad - hormones!"

For some reason those few words from a complete stranger rattled around in my brain constantly during those first couple of VERY HARD weeks. I dismissed everything I was experiencing as 'typical hormone issues.' That first night in the hospital after delivering, I literally couldn't speak to my best friend on the phone without crying. Tears streamed down my face and I sobbed out every word. I remember apologizing, "I'm . . . sorry . . . I . . . can't . . . stop . . . crying . . . hormones . . ." She remembers that conversation, too. It was a little unsettling but also, yeah, she admitted "hormones" made sense. When I had my hardest cry on the way home from the hospital, I chalked it up to those crazy hormones doing their thang. When I sat in my green rocker/recliner, unable to sit up without assistance, sobbing whenever I had the chance to be alone? Hormones. This would all go away as soon as I could get my hormones to even out. If only I could breastfeed. That was supposed to help equalize things, wasn't it? Or did it just help my uterus contract? I couldn't remember. I was wallowing in sadness because *my hormones* were causing all of my problems. Right? Eventually I'd "snap out of it."

Right?

Have you seen the cartoon by Robot Hugs about if we treated physical diseases the way that we treat mental illnesses? [9]

(continued on next page)

---

[9]Printed with permission. http://www.robot-hugs.com/helpful-advice/

I knew that the numbness, anxiety, and the frustration was extreme, unlike anything I had experienced before. But I'd also never birthed a child before. And I kept hearing that "baby blues" were inevitable. So I just needed to fight through the inevitable.

The only problem was, I didn't feel like fighting.

I didn't feel like being there at all.

Not just being in the bedroom, struggling to recover from surgery. Not just in the apartment, struggling to be a mother.

I didn't want to be anywhere. I didn't want to exist. Dying didn't sound so bad.

In fact, being dead sounded like a lovely break.

Chapter 13

Death Wishes

"Did you ever want to kill yourself?"

That's a question people ask a lot when they find out you were depressed. I think that very question is a large part of the reason postpartum depression is such a taboo subject. It's scary. Very scary. But it's an important topic to broach. I think that many women don't want to admit that they have PPD, or they don't want people to know about it, because of the horror stories that postpartum psychosis can produce. Those stories are the ones that the general public hears. We always hear about the worst of the worst cases. They are what grab media attention. Remember that mom of five who drowned all of her children in the bathtub? Or that woman who drove her car off a bridge, with her two children fastened in the backseat? Or the one who thought the president was trying to harm her so she drove her car toward the White House, over barricades, until she was shot to death while her infant daughter sat in a carseat in the back of the car? What about the woman who left a note apologizing for ruining her child's life by accidentally dropping him? In order to prevent a lifetime of perceived struggle she jumped out a window with him in her arms. Her baby survived because her body provided a cushion from the fall. She did not.

I remember hearing about the woman who drowned her children in the bathtub when I was in college. I remember the outrage surrounding the story. The general sentiment was incredulous. How could someone be such a monster? There was even a profile in People magazine. The common denominator in all of these stories is that the mother suffered from "postpartum depression." At least, that is how the media reported it. They tossed around the idea that being depressed led to these actions and, yes, it may have started that way. But postpartum psychosis and postpartum depression are two very different diagnoses. Very different realities. Who wants to hear about that though? The nuanced differences, both quiet and loud? Not the media. They're too afraid that you've already clicked over to the latest celebrity scandal so they use the broad term "postpartum depression" without explaining further. Those of us who are quietly suffering from postpartum depression—actual postpartum depression, which comes in many forms—keep our heads down and power through because we don't want to be associated with these extreme cases.

If I could have stood up on my own, I wonder if I would have actually left? Walked out the door "to get milk," as the cliché goes, and never come back. I certainly fantasized about it, the idea of leaving my apartment and creating an alternate world where I wasn't Meagan anymore and I certainly wasn't a mother. I'd live a quiet existence, under the radar, the shame of my secret past bubbling under the surface. People would wonder what my story was—where I came from, who my family was—but they would never know because I would never tell. I'd be in some out of the way small town, living in a trailer, and quietly waiting tables at the local diner. I'd wonder how Dan and Owen were doing, maybe. But mostly I'd shut my mind to that world so I didn't have to deal with the pain. It would be a total break from reality. Almost like a split personality. I'd convince myself that the world I left never existed in the first place. Then maybe I'd find some sort of happiness again.

Was this my only fantasy? No I imagined other scenarios, too. I imagined what it would be like to simply not exist. It didn't seem like the worst thing in the world if I was in some sort of car accident. If my car hit a tree, but I could still get out, maybe I just . . . wouldn't. Maybe I could just let myself go.

So did I want to kill myself?

Not in the conventional sense of wanting to slit my wrists or hang myself or find a gun or take a bunch of pills. But if I *happened* to find myself in a situation where my life was in danger? Slipping away didn't seem like such a bad thing. I wasn't going to actually put myself in danger, but I did think about how simply not existing would be a relief.

> **Doctor's Note:**
>
> Preoccupation with suicidal thoughts is referred to as 'suicidal ideation' in the mental health community. Most people who have suicidal thoughts do not attempt suicide, however, it is important to take these thoughts seriously. One important distinguishing question as to the seriousness of these thoughts is whether the person has a plan on how, when, and where to execute their suicide or whether he or she simply fantasizes that they are no longer around.
>
> - Abigail Levrini, Ph.D.

I learned through treatment that those kinds of thoughts are known as "death wishes." Death wishes are passive suicidal tendencies, instead of active. Even though passive suicidal thoughts, like wanting to die in one's sleep or develop a terminal illness or get in a car accident, allow a bit more time for intervention, some doctors caution that they are equally concerning[10]. Passive thoughts can become active thoughts rather quickly and unexpectedly.

It makes me feel so unbelievably sad to think that I could have let myself slip away. I had lost my urge to fight. And I'm a fighter.

---

[10] http://www.currentpsychiatry.com/the-publication/issue-single-view/passive-suicidal-ideation-still-a-high-risk-clinical-scenario/651a76321f5ec282d271b194343a9bfd.html

When I was fifteen I had a severe allergic reaction to over-the-counter painkillers I was taking for menstrual cramps and a sore throat. I went into anaphylactic shock at school when I was in the tenth grade. I started breaking out in hives while taking an exam so I went to the nurse's office, excited I was going to be able to miss the test. The nurse called my mom to come pick me up and I went back to my classroom to get my backpack. As I walked back to the office, I started to see black spots. I made it to the nurse, told her what I was seeing and she told me to lie down. That was the last thing I heard. The next thing I knew I was on the ground and she was shouting for someone to call 911. By the time my mom and my sister arrived, I was on the ground. I could hear them, but I couldn't see them. They told me later that my eyes were open the whole time. I was temporarily blind. When the paramedics arrived, my pulse was so low that they couldn't find it manually. They inserted oxygen tubes into my nose, put me on a gurney, and wheeled me out to the ambulance. I knew my parents were following in my dad's car. Then my throat completely closed, and I knew that was it. I was going to die.

The paramedics threw an oxygen mask on me, then pumped me full of Benadryl and epinephrine. Suddenly I could breathe again. I started to stabilize. Lying in my hospital bed, I couldn't stop scratching myself because of the epinephrine and I couldn't keep my eyes open because of the Benadryl. My doctor thought I was sleeping and I heard him say to the nurse, "She's lucky. I've seen cases this bad where they don't come out of it." I decided then and there that every moment was a gift. That life can be gone in an instant and I'm going to fight for every moment.

Fifteen years later and I was in another fight for my life.

But I had lost the will to fight on.

Chapter 14

Things I Wish

1. I wish I had recognized the shift in myself sooner.

2. I wish I allowed myself to show others that something was wrong.

3. I wish there wasn't such a stigma surrounding PPD. Maybe someone would have said something to me earlier.

4. I wish that OB/GYNs were *required* to distribute a list of qualified, local psychiatrists available for all patients, along with the other physical self-care guidelines that are given out post-birth.

5. I wish that every new mother had a strong network of women surrounding them—brand new mothers like themselves with whom to share their experiences, mothers with several kids to offer

perspective, and grandmothers who could provide comfort and reprieve when needed.

6. I wish that I hadn't assumed that PPD wouldn't happen to me. Maybe I would have learned more about it and understood the signs better. Maybe I wouldn't have gone so long without help.

7. I wish people would think before asking, "Are you just loving being a mom?" to new mothers still raw from the birthing/adjusting experience.

8. I wish we could all be a little more honest about the realities of parenthood—especially new parenthood—and not expect for everything to be rosy. It's hard work and it really does, as the cliché goes, "change everything."

Chapter 15

Jes and Heather

My friend Mike and I were in improv classes together. Mike looks like a classic jock from an eighties movie, but he's got a sharp sense of humor, a quick wit, and an eager-to-please disposition that seems incongruent with his appearance. There was a group of us who took several levels of improv training together and often we'd go out after class for drinks and eats. We'd talk about class and get to know each other better, important to do when working without a net in the comedy world. Several times on these "after school" outings Mike told me I had to meet his wife, Jes. He thought we'd really get along. I'd say, "I'd love to," and I meant it. But I also figured it was something people just said to be nice. The chances that his wife and I would actually hang out seemed slim. Classes end. People go in different directions.

At the end of July 2012, we were in the Keys with my family on our annual trip and I finally revealed that we were having a baby. We had gathered all the extended family for a photo to mark the start of the trip. My brother (who we had told a few hours earlier) was taking rapid-fire shots with the camera as I said, "Ok everyone! On the count of three say, 'Meagan's Pregnant!'" It was a pretty fun way to reveal the big news. Later that day I was scrolling through Twitter, and saw that Mike had just tweeted something like, "Holy crap I'm going to be a dad!" I immediately gushed my excitement to him through Twitter in a few characters. When he said that his wife was due in March I was genuinely excited. We would know other parents in LA with babies the same age. But I didn't tell him that I was pregnant yet. It was still early on and we wanted to wait to tell our friends until after the first trimester.

In the next level of improv classes Mike was in a different class. But we did a few practice groups together and kept in touch through social media. Two weeks after Owen was born, to the day, Mike's daughter was born. Mike posted the the play-by-play on Facebook; I followed along from my rocker-recliner as they went to the hospital and the baby was born. I was deep in my fog of misery. I tweeted things like, "Now that I have a newborn, I wash my hands like a surgeon." And Mike would 'favorite' these little tidbits because this was his new reality, too.

A few weeks after Mike and Jes's daughter was born, I received an invite for a "Housewarming/Meet P" party at their house. Their place was a good half hour from where we lived, and any sort of excursion outside our immediate radius sounded like an insurmountable event. Dan doesn't love going to places where he has to socialize with people he doesn't really know. I was two months into being a mother and socializing was low on my list of desires as well. But I had a hunch that if we didn't go to this party, we'd likely never meet up with Mike and Jes. And it seemed important to know other parents.

Call it a mother's intuition.

* * * * *

We gathered all our stuff. I found a Dr. Seuss book that we had a duplicate of, one that Owen actually seemed to listen to at this early stage, and inscribed it as a gift for P. Then we headed west.

We were among the first to arrive. One of Mike's friends was there, but that was it. Jes was in the kitchen setting up tacos and I needed to put together a bottle for Owen. There's a shorthand that sometimes passes between new moms, especially when you sense that not all is roses and dandelions. We skipped over the normal "aren't you loving it?" bullshit and landed immediately on the real stuff: the trials of breastfeeding.When she saw that I was putting together formula, the floodgates opened. I remember very distinctly standing in the threshold of their kitchen door, leaning in to one another, almost conspiratorially trading our stories.

Turns out she had already had mastitis, a painful infection from blocked ducts in the breast, three times since P was born. Her breasts were swollen and infected and she was miserable. She was pumping to try to continue breastfeeding because, as we've all heard over and over, "breast is best." I told her that I was hardly producing any milk, and that I was pumping and supplementing with formula because Owen would only latch on every once in awhile. Suddenly it felt like we both had permission. Permission to formula feed when necessary, and permission to admit how hard it can be for some mothers. We talked about how much we were crying. I told her I had just cut all my hair off because who had time to deal with hair when there's a little human demanding all of your time? And she was like, "Yes! I want to do that, too. It would be so much easier." In those first few moments of their housewarming party, I was the one feeling much warmer. I had just met a kindred spirit who was going through the exact same trials at the exact same time. It was a relief to not feel so alone.

Jes told me her friend Heather, who also had a newborn, would be at the party, too. When she arrived I recognized her immediately. We were both at a Huggies print audition in January, and I remembered her because, a) you check out your competition at these things, b) she is a stunningly beautiful blonde who I assumed would get cast over me and c) because it was a quiet room and I unintentionally heard her tell someone about how she and her boyfriend were together only a short amount of time before she got pregnant. I'm such a nosy nit. Turns out, neither of us got cast in that print ad. And she showed up with her best friend, not her boyfriend. Her best friend, Laura, worked with Jes, which is how they all knew each other. Heather's daughter, A., was crying when they got there so she headed straight back to P.'s nursery to nurse. Heather was frazzled because A. hadn't napped all day. They spent most of the party in that back bedroom and I felt awkward approaching Heather because I didn't really know her and crying babies sent my anxiety levels through the roof at that point, so I didn't talk to Heather much that first night. I did find out, however, that Owen and A. were born one day apart. That was pretty neat. Before the party ended, the three of us decided we should try to get together soon. Suddenly, I was really glad we didn't skip out on the evening.

* * * * *

When I've shared my struggles with new moms who are also struggling, I always ask them if they have any mom friends. More specifically, I ask if they have found mom friends whose babies are the same age as their children. I truly believe that having Jes and Heather in my life that first year is part of why I was able to cope, why I didn't completely implode. We became each other's sounding boards and checkpoints and hand-holders and "me-too'ers" and "you-too's??" The three of us faced very different challenges for various reasons. We were parenting differently. We had three incredibly different children. But instead of those differences driving us apart, they brought us closer because we were open to hearing each other, to learning from each other. We were also open to the idea that our children's needs were different, and we needed to mother to our specific child's needs. Jes was going to school and working evenings as a bartender, so she was struggling to balance being a student, a provider, and a mother. Heather had fallen into attachment parenting so her daughter was constantly at her hip or breast or bedside, not because that was what she always intended to do but because that was what her child needed. I was dealing with depression, even though I wasn't quite aware of it yet. We shared our experiences and advice and took away what was best for our babies. But best of all, we shared our time. We had companions who understood what we were going through. Since our babies were the same age, any time we got together they were pretty much going through the same stages, doing similar things. That meant that we could actually talk. It's helpful to have a mom friend that has a two-year-old when you have a two-month-old. It's great that they've "been there" and can let you know that things get easier. But they're likely also telling you about their experiences while running after a toddler and answering "why? why? why?" questions and taking potty-training breaks. Jes, Heather, and I were lucky. Our babies were in sync. Which meant we could be in sync with one another.

Our first outing as a six-some was to a "mommy and me" movie at the Grove. The Grove is an outdoor mall in LA, right across the street from where I lived. Every Monday at the movie theater, the 11am of the latest release was a "mommy and me" showing. They set up a stroller parking area in the lobby and changing table inside the theater. You didn't have to worry if your baby cried the whole time. Guess what? There'd be another baby crying, too. And you could walk up and down the aisle, soothing your babe, while still watching a movie meant for grownups, not just another cartoon. On that first outing we saw "Superman." The movie was pretty loud and perhaps not the best for our newborns, but it felt like such an important step for us to get together for the first time after the party. Unfortunately, I was super hungry afterward and I didn't stay to hang out much past the movie's end. Then I beat myself up on the walk home about leaving abruptly. I almost turned around after being gone for ten minutes but then I felt like a desperate weirdo. I hardly knew these women. What would it have looked like if I was suddenly back after insisting I needed to get home to eat? Instead of turning around, I decided to send a text saying that I wished I could have stayed longer and hoped we could all get together again soon. For the record, when I later confessed my urge to come back that day they both insisted that they wouldn't have thought twice about it.

Which brings me to my next point. Sometimes you will be that desperate weirdo when you're a new mom. Finding those mom friends with babies the same age, means that you can be the desperate weirdo in the company of other understanding women. And that is priceless. There's a video that went viral a little while ago that perfectly illustrates the friendship dance of new moms. There's a mom watching another mom on the playground. She thinks the other mom has it all together, and she wishes she could be like her. She wonders if it would be weird if she said hello. She almost talks herself out of it. Then the other mom drops something and she goes to help her pick it up. She sees that the other mom has big stain on her shirt, and realizes that she's just as "messed up" as she is. Then the two women decide to get coffee, and basically skip off into the sunset.

It takes a lot of persistence and patience to be friends with a new mom. There are large swaths of time that can pass before a text is answered, because answering means putting down a baby that cries hysterically every time he's put down. New moms are going to be late nine times out of ten because their baby had a blow out before walking out the door. And if they're not late, they might cancel because their baby *finally* decided to take a nap right before you're supposed to meet up. But all of that is okay because it's a two-way street and you're often the one with the hiccups in your schedule. You guys get each other. Having that understanding is clutch in those early days. So chat up that mom on the playground who looks intimidatingly cool.

Chances are she's thinking the same thing about you.

Chapter 16

Keeping Busy

I learned when Owen was only a few months old that Los
Angeles has an embarrassment of riches for a new mother
desperately seeking distraction. You can keep busy if you really want
to. And I wanted to. Sitting in my apartment while Owen sat in his
swing or laid on the rug or bounced in his bouncy seat was not really
an option. I felt like I couldn't take my eyes off of him (heyyy,
Anxiety) so it's not like I could get anything done at home. Instead, I
would start sliding down the rabbit hole of unhealthy thoughts and I
didn't want to go there. I didn't want to think about the loneliness or
regret or sadness or nothingness or disappointment. God, no.

To save myself from all of that thinking, I clung desperately to my new mama friends. I accepted any invite they extended. I also signed up for Red Tricycle, an email list about kid-friendly activities going on in the area.

Monday was movie day. Every Monday I'd walk across the street to see the latest release. Sometimes Jes and Heather would join, like they did for "Superman," but often it was just Owen and me. This was fine. Going to the movies was a form of escape and I welcomed that escape with open arms.

Tuesdays was "Mommy and Me" yoga, and I didn't miss a week if I could help it. I absolutely loved the instructor, Victoria. She gave the babies such freedom to explore and us mamas the space to just breathe for an hour. There was always a period in the beginning of class when we would go around and introduce our babies and ourselves, and say one milestone or challenge from the past week. There was also time at the end of the class to connect with other mothers before we faced the world alone again. I loved the communal space that Victoria fostered.

Wednesdays were museum days. From 9-10am, the Zimmerman Children's Museum had VIB Hour—Very Important Baby. For that hour on Wednesdays the museum was only open to children ages two and under, so that's where Owen and I would be. The museum has various play stations—ball pits, water tables, a little cafe, and a grocery store. Some mornings they offered music class. It was basically a sensory dream for little ones. Owen loved it. We slowly started seeing familiar faces each week, and developed a friendly rapport with our fellow "regulars." It was a great place to spend a morning. If I was lucky, he'd play hard enough that he'd fall asleep on the walk back home.

On wild card days, usually Thursday mornings, we'd wander over to the park in the community where we lived. There was an informal group of parents and kids that showed up between 10am and noon on weekdays to hang. Everyone brought toys for their kids and everyone else's kids to play with. It was an unspoken agreement that everyone brought extra toys to make sure there were enough to share. We'd sit in the shade while the kids played in the dirt, shared toys, ran, and crawled around. The kids ranged from newborn to about four years old. It was casual. Just come as you are and hang out. I'd make a point to get over there at least once a week.

Indoor play spaces are also big in LA. There was a great one near where Jes and Heather lived. It was a bit of a hike for me, but I'd always happily meet them over there. The Magic Forest is exactly that. Magic. It's a Waldorf-inspired play space, clean and bright, with wooden toys and a sweet wooden playhouse in the middle. It's all cream and light wood, not the typical primary color assault you get in most "children's" places. There's a coffee bar for parents and we would sip away the afternoons, letting the babies explore while we chatted. There was a place called "Books and Cookies;" the name alone was too much for me to resist. They offered a great music class on Fridays and a program where you could drop off your child for supervised play-time while you stayed just outside the playroom in the cafe. Jes and I took advantage of this a few times. It was a rare time for her to squeeze in school-work and for me to get some writing done.

And if we weren't at one of these haunts you'd find us in the backyard, playing with leaves. Or we'd walk over to the La Brea Tar Pits and wander the lawns or watch the scientists excavate at the observation pit.

I didn't allow myself much downtime. It was a strategic move on my part. I avoided what was really going on in my head. I probably wouldn't have been able to go on as long as I did without seeking help, had I not forced all of these distractions. I pulled a Dory and floated along singing, "just keep swimming." If I stopped moving, the reality of this great divide within would become clearer. So instead I'd shake it off and keep moving. Staying busy is a common coping mechanism. It's a way to mask how you're actually feeling. It's fairly easy to do when you're too busy to notice. At least it is in my family. My grandmother is one of the busiest people I know and she's in her eighties. Ever since my grandfather passed away, she's kept herself occupied with various church activities and committees, lunches with friends, trips to see her extended family all over Florida and Georgia. One time a few years after Owen was born, I commented to her about how she kept so busy and she responded, "Well, yes. Better to stay busy than to sit around the house. Because then I start thinking . . . " I understood what that hanging ellipses meant. If you stop moving, the sadness has a chance to seep through the floorboards of your mind.

But let's be real, you gotta keep busy in those early days, months, year. Babies can be frightfully boring. For awhile all they do is cry, eat, and poop. And you're stuck just kind of wondering . . .

Is this it?

Chapter 17

Realizing

Picking up the phone and saying, "I need to talk to someone about my postpartum depression" was one of the hardest things I've ever done. It was also one of the most courageous.

It took nine months after Owen's birth to even recognize that something was wrong. I just thought the way that I felt—or didn't feel—was my new reality. That sometimes life doesn't turn out how you think it will and, as a result, the cloud that was pushing me down, weighing heavy on my heart and my shoulders and my head —a literal pressure that made me gasp for breath sometimes—was what I was left to deal with.

I couldn't be depressed. I had a new baby. He was healthy and beautiful and full of energy. I had an amazing husband who was helpful with diapers and dishes, and gave my baby and me sweet kisses. I was living my dream of being an actress and a writer and a mother. How dare I, even for a moment, feel anything other than bliss?

But what I learned during those dark months is that depression doesn't discriminate. It doesn't care if everything is lined up in your life, if you've hit all the points on your checklist for optimum happiness. It doesn't make sense to those looking in from the outside who have never felt it. And in those dark times, having never dealt with depression before, it didn't make sense to me either. But it didn't matter. Suddenly I was being held down under the water by an unseen cosmic hand, unable to breathe and unable to scream. Like the classic nightmare when you open your mouth and nothing comes out. But instead of panic, I just felt a sense of defeat . . . and acceptance. No one could hear me screaming, but it didn't matter because nothing mattered to me at the time. If I suddenly didn't exist any more, it wouldn't even be a blip in the grand scheme of the universe. I just wanted to quietly disappear.

In November, nine months after Owen was born, a friend and a family member, both became mothers for the first time. While I'm sure they faced their own private struggles, on social media they posted happy-looking pictures with their babies, with captions proclaiming their joy. Being a mom was the "best thing that had ever happened to them." And I was *pissed*. Anger was one of the few emotions I still felt. I was livid that they were such liars. "Best" thing? More like the worst thing. Motherhood had stripped me of my happiness, not given me more of it. Why would they so blatantly lie about something like that? Why not just post cute pictures and leave the lying captions out of it? But through my seething anger, something shifted. I had something like a realization. From buried deep in my psyche, a small voice whispered, "What if they're not lying? What if they actually *are* happy? And if they are, why aren't you?"

Around that same time I was cleaning out my sock drawer, throwing away ones with holes in them, taking inventory of what I needed for the winter, when I saw a pair of fuzzy pink, purple, and white striped socks stuffed in the back corner. They had a little pink peace sign embroidered on the ankle. I had forgotten about them. I had gotten them from Target and packed them dutifully in my hospital bag when we were preparing for Owen's arrival. I read somewhere that it gets cold in the hospital and fuzzy slipper socks are a good item to bring. Those socks never made it out of my hospital bag. Nothing I packed in preparation for our hospital stay made it out of my hospital bag. Somehow seeing those socks crammed in the far back corner, hiding from everyday view, was a trigger that November. They reminded me that I'd once been happy and excited about becoming a mother. I bought them in anticipation of a season filled with joy and love. Now they reminded me that nothing had turned out how I anticipated.

When I saw those socks I actually recoiled. I had never had that kind of reaction to a physical object before. It was like the socks were a talisman for all broken dreams and it was too painful to confront. There was my naïveté staring me in the face: Fuzzy, pink, and hopeful.

And that's when it hit me. I wasn't happy. I hadn't felt happiness in a long time. When was the last time I was happy??

I couldn't remember.

Chapter 18

Getting Help

On November 14, 2013 at 10am, I wrote the following. This is the raw cut, verbatim and untouched, from the moment I first reached beyond the bubble of my mind.

* * * * *

It's been 8 1/2 months since Owen was born. And just now, for the first time, I picked up the phone and called a therapist. I have stress sweat just from leaving a message. And I'm in the land of therapy . . . everyone I know has a therapist and still there is a stigma attached in my brain. I've never asked for help like this before. I've always powered through. And it's taken me the better part of a year to finally make this call. How many women don't make the call?

After Owen was born, I couldn't stop crying. And yet, at the same time, I felt completely numb. Where was the bliss I was supposed to feel after becoming a mom? Where was the overwhelming love? In retrospect, I get it. I experienced a physical trauma that my mind and body needed to heal from. Pushing for seven hours and ending up with a c-section anyway was not the way I had envisioned any of this going down. I was on no sleep and there was no sleep in sight. I had had major abdominal surgery and I'm allergic to most painkillers. The ones they could give me made me feel worse so I stuck with Tylenol. TYLENOL ONLY AFTER SURGERY. Can you imagine? All while trying to nurse and care for a new person. I couldn't care for myself. Who was I to expect that I could care for him? But this is all in retrospect. In the moment, I felt guilt, anger, fear, pain, anxiety...the list goes on. And now, 8 1/2 months later, I still feel residual guilt and waves of sadness that come out of seemingly nowhere.

So I'm finally getting help so that I can get past this. Because for the most part now, I love being Owen's mom. And one day I'd like to give him a sibling. But there is no way I can even think about it until I address the scars I acquired when I brought him into the world.

One of the most frustrating things about dealing with the aftershocks of childbirth has been the lack of support I've been able to find. I called my OB/GYN to see if she recommended any therapists that specialize in postpartum issues. Her nurse called me back and said I had to call the number on my insurance card. Well no shit. I'd already done research online through my insurance provider. Eleven pages came up with psychologists that are covered. Eleven. It'd be nice to have that list narrowed down a bit, especially since it's difficult to find reviews or personal websites for any of these therapists.

A month or so ago, I finally felt strong enough to read Brooke Shields' book Down Came the Rain about her struggle with postpartum depression. I had definitely heard of it but the idea of reading about anyone else's experience just seemed to depress me more. But it'd been half a year since Owen came along, so I felt like I could read it objectively. But you know what? I checked it out from the library and scurried around like a little mouse, afraid someone might see me looking for it. And when I couldn't find it, I finally asked the librarian and she took me to where it was, picked it up and read the subtitle aloud. My embarrassment was then off the charts. I had O in his stroller so I clearly was getting this book for myself. She then asked me if I had heard of a postpartum support group that a friend of hers had started in LA. I looked up the name of it when I got home but can't remember it now.

Reading Brooke's book made me realize that I should talk to someone. I was reading passages aloud to my husband because it felt like I could have written it myself. I had such similar experiences and emotions and I finally realized that I wasn't alone. That I shouldn't be so ashamed. And that I couldn't just push those experiences out of my mind because I was feeling better now. They keep bubbling up unexpectedly and I need to learn how to cope with them.

* * * * *

I vividly remember when the librarian read that subtitle "My Journey through Postpartum Depression" aloud. A few years later, after getting the help I so desperately needed, I'm quite open about my postpartum struggles. Obviously, since I've *written my own book about it*. But at that point in my life? Standing in a public library with my infant son, trying to find a book about postpartum depression? I was ashamed and mortified to think that I could possibly be struggling with something that was "supposed" to come so naturally. But more than that, I was worried that people would know I was even interested in reading a book on PPD. When the librarian looked at me with empathetic eyes and asked me if I had heard of her friend's support group, I thought it was a kind gesture but I was too ashamed to take her advice at the time. I looked up the name of the group, but that was it. I didn't do anything beyond that.

And I remember reading passages of Brooke's book aloud to Dan. I'd been pretty open with Dan about all I was going through ever since the beginning. He's my trench mate in this war, after all. But I was usually dismissive with the *weight* of what I was going through. I used humor to mask the gravity of how I felt, both to him and myself. And we laughed together about it. He knew how much most of this new parenthood thing sucked. He was there. He saw. He worked from home. He heard the crying. Mine and Owen's. He felt the shift in our world. But both of us were uneducated and uninformed about depression. We didn't realize that all the signs of needing help were there. It's not something our society communicates about openly.

If you're not feeling well physically, there is usually a list of symptoms available to help you diagnose yourself. Does your throat hurt? Are you nauseated? Do you have a fever? Aches? Chills? Depending on the answer, there's likely a medicine to help you cope with your symptoms. We didn't even think to *look* for a checklist of symptoms about postpartum depression. It wasn't on our radar. PPD was something that happened to other people, people who had dealt with depression before or had other kinds of mental struggles.

It wasn't until reading Brooke Shields' book that I had my 'a-ha' moment. I was dancing around my realization but it wasn't until hearing Brooke's words echo the ones I had either spoken aloud to Dan like, "I made a terrible mistake," or "I hate myself and I hate my life," [11]. Or thoughts I had written down in secret like, "Why would anyone want to do this more than once?"[12] Or thoughts that I kept trapped inside about how I finally understood why or how friends had taken their own lives. She also admitted that she understood how a close friend must have felt before committing suicide.

She too had an easy pregnancy, without morning sickness, feeling great the whole time through. She was also knocked sideways by the idea of being depressed because when her doctor asked if she had a history of depression, she had "never experienced anything beyond melancholy and the occasional low period that can be a part of life . . . No matter how sad I felt, I could always find a

---

[11] *Down Came the Rain*, pg 98

[12] *Down Came the Rain*, pg 70

way to overcome it and not be destroyed. In my wildest dreams, I never thought I could fall so far."[13]

Depression felt like something that happened to "other" people.

It wasn't until I saw my journey reflected through her journey that I started to wake up.

---

[13] *Down Came the Rain,* pgs 139-40

Chapter 19

Revisiting

We do what we can to get through each day. For me, sweeping realities to the side has always been an easy coping mechanism. There's no doubt that being an actress and a writer have helped feed my habit. Slipping into a different skin through acting and creating new worlds through my fingertips while I write can help perpetuate my powers of denial. I had to bring Owen along with me to therapy twice when we were in LA. Dan was traveling and I couldn't find anyone to watch O during my appointment. Scratch that. I *wouldn't* find anyone. I had a lot of difficulty letting anyone watch him. Anxiety out the wazoo. So I brought him with me, which my therapist suggested when I told her Dan was out of town during our next session. Owen is a ridiculously happy kid. He goes with the flow, loves new people, and has an infectious giggle. This threw my therapist for a loop. "He's so happy," she said with an incredulous tone, as he explored her office, grabbing everything within reach. "Yep," I replied, nonplussed. "It's really remarkable," she said. "I've seen babies whose mothers are depressed, who are the saddest little creatures you've ever seen. Just serious and sad. You must have been very good at hiding your depression." "I'm a really good actress," I replied. And, until that moment, I don't think I realized the truth of that statement. It's something you have to believe in order to deal with the mountains of rejection this industry throws at you. But I never thought about how I applied my acting skills to my real life. Yet there it was, reflected in little human form.

Happiness.

And I hadn't felt truly happy in months. Which I'd realize after going on medication and that familiar feeling crept back in.

Chapter 20

Babies are the Worst

I was sitting in traffic at Third and Formosa, trying to get to the light at La Brea so I could turn left. I don't remember where I was going. I don't remember if Owen was with me. But I do remember seeing a woman walking west along the sidewalk, pushing a stroller and juggling a toddler in her arms. She was trying to fix the blanket that had been shielding the baby in the stroller from the sun. She was slightly off balance and the attempt was not effortless. I mumbled to myself, full of disdain and pity, "Babies are the worst." And I meant it. They ruined your life. Your ability to function. I didn't bat an eye at my assessment. Now that I've received treatment and feel back to my "normal" self, I reflect upon the bitterness that pretty much oozed from my pores and it absolutely feels like I'm looking at a different person.

All my life, I've been a baby magnet. I loved babies and babies loved me. There was a baby in the room? Gimme. I wanted to hold and snuggle and coo. And on more occasions than I can count, babies would reach for me. Babies of strangers, babies of friends, babies of family. Gimme. So it was a true wake-up call when I met my cousin's daughter at Owen's first Christmas.

Little Piper was born six months after Owen and was all of four months old when the holidays rolled around. She's my cousin Tatum's first baby and the first grandbaby for my Aunt Lindi, my mom's sister. We always celebrate Christmas Eve with my mom's side of the family and there was an extra buzz of excitement since this would be a "first" for so many. I had started seeing my therapist at this point and was planning to talk to my parents on this trip about that decision. There was a lot going on. We were looking to make a cross-country move from Los Angeles to Florida, I was finally confronting my depression, and now it was Christmas, the most anticipated and stress-inducing holiday of the year. There were a lot of balls in the air. Would everyone get there in time to eat and get to church? It's family tradition for my mom to make her famous lasagna on Christmas Eve. Dan doesn't eat pasta. We usually whip chicken parmesan together for him. My cousin was bringing a friend who didn't eat meat. A meatless sauce was prepared for her. My uncle and his wife were coming for the first time in maybe fifteen years. There were two babies experiencing their first Christmas, two cousins experiencing their first Christmas as parents, and two sets of new grandparents.

Owen was trying to walk (and would end up being an official walker a few weeks later) so he needed constant supervision. I was on edge even more than usual. My parents' house was far from baby-proofed. Everything was a potential trap—from the holiday decorations to the entertainment center to the open dock leading to the canal in the backyard. No amount of wine was going to help ease the hyper-alert-jittery-mania I was experiencing. My eyes kept darting quickly from side to side, assessing the dangers Owen might encounter. I'm sure that to the outside world I seemed fine, but everything was bubbling under the surface like an underwater volcano. The slightest shift in my tectonic plates would cause an inevitable eruption.

That shift was sparked by a tiny, sweet baby girl.

I looked at Piper, and I couldn't remember Owen being that small. Ever. But the way her fingers moved felt familiar. The alien-ish pointing and flexing, constantly moving and grasping and intertwining, together and apart. And the gurgles and coos and sighs and little cries sounded familiar. And "familiar" did not mean "good." I clearly did not have positive associations with this time. I wanted to run away. I wanted to walk out the door and not look back. I could feel my breath catching when I looked at her. But I played the part of supportive and excited cousin. "She's so sweet!" I exclaimed. I gave her my finger to hold. I remarked on her tiny feet and soft skin. And then, oh no, gotta go, Owen is gonna pull over that wooden reindeer. I avoided Piper as much as I could by playing the part of attentive mother.

Then Tatum asked where she could change Piper's diaper. I took her to the back bedroom and paused to chat. I wanted to know how Tatum was really feeling, hoping to find an ally. Someone struggling as much as me. "It's hard, isn't it?" I asked. "Yeah," she replied as she changed her daughter. "But she's so great. And such an easy baby." She was being honest; I could tell. This made me even sadder. I was alone again. And then the moment I had been dreading. I was wallowing in self-pity when Tatum asked innocently, "Do you want to hold her?"

I was screaming internally. I wanted nothing to do with Piper and her sweet little hands and sweet little squeals and sweet little drools. I felt a tightness in my chest and I was having difficulty breathing. I had gone down too deep and the pressure was squeezing me on all sides, inside and out. But the show must go on.

"Sure," I smiled. Then I was holding her. What had always felt like the most natural thing in my life—a baby in my arms— suddenly felt like the most foreign. She felt like a sack of sugar and I had no connection at all. I somehow kept up conversation, about what I don't know and then she started to fuss and, phew, I had found

my out and I handed her back to her mother.

Holy shit. This was way worse than I realized.

Smiling for everyone, but crumbling inside.

Before I left for the holidays, my therapist asked me to

consider going on depression medication. It seemed ridiculous. I

didn't think I was *currently* depressed. I just wanted to talk to someone about the dark month that immediately followed Owen's birth. I felt like I might have some "unresolved issues" regarding how it all went down and if I just talked about these issues with someone, then I'd be able to crawl my way out of them. I wasn't going to start meds. She told me just to think about it so we could discuss more when I got back, but suggested that I make an appointment with a psychiatrist just to hold a spot. I could always cancel if I wanted to. If she ended up prescribing me something, I didn't have to take it.

It was on Christmas Eve, standing in my parents hallway, fighting back tears and swallowing my volcano, that I realized I would not be canceling my appointment.

Chapter 21

Feeling Happy Again

(Owen, 11 months old)

I didn't want to take medicine. I didn't think things were bad enough to warrant medication. I didn't know anyone in my immediate circle of family and friends who took medicine for their mental health. If I did, it wasn't something that people I knew talked about so I wasn't aware. Medicine was for "other" people, those not strong enough to power through and straighten themselves out on their own. I saw medicine as a sign of weakness instead of a way back to strength. I thought that if I could talk through my experiences, I would start to feel lighter again. I thought I could dig myself out, session by session, and find equilibrium again. Christmas made me realize how bad things really were. Talking my way out of depression didn't seem as likely anymore, and that scared me to death.

I went to my first psychiatrist appointment with a list of questions.

How long would I need to be on the medication?

How easy is it to wean off the medication?

What are the side effects of the medication?

How long would it take for the medication to start working?

Would I have to be on meds for the rest of my life?

Before I started asking my questions, she started asking hers.

What brought you in today?

How are the sessions going with your psychologist?

Do you feel comfortable with her?

Do you want to continue meeting with her as you receive treatment?

What is your medical history?

Does anyone in your family suffer from depression?

Have you ever struggled with depression?

Do you want to kill yourself?

Are you willing to take medication?

When I started answering her questions, the floodgates opened. I hadn't cried in a long time; now I couldn't stop. I felt broken and defeated. I wanted help to get back on my feet. I was relieved to learn that, most likely, I would only need to be on medication for ten-to-twelve months. Given the acute nature of my depressive episode, my psychiatrist felt I'd be able to "reset" in a minimal amount of time. She planned to start me on a low dosage and then check in a month later to see how I felt. I would likely need to increase my dosage to a higher amount, but I should be able to detect differences within two weeks or so. I left feeling cautiously optimistic. Maybe this could work. Maybe I hadn't been doled out a life sentence of misery. Maybe change could happen.

I talked to Dan when I got home and told him I thought I should try the medication. He had helped me compile the list of questions for the psychiatrist before my appointment so we went over what I learned. We are both skeptical about medication in general. We're not ones to pop a pill at the first hint of a headache. Often we'll tough it out or sleep it away. This was new territory for us. Neither of us had ever sought help for a psychological condition so we were understandably apprehensive. But he lived with me. He knew how much I was struggling. He was struggling too. He didn't know how to make me happy again. Feeling helpless when your spouse needs help is incredibly difficult. A few years earlier Dan had experienced a series of medical setbacks and we still don't have all the answers. We saw a myriad of specialists, often more than one of each. We were searching for answers to make him well again and often came up empty. It is still one of the hardest things we've dealt with in our marriage. All I wanted was a magic answer to help him feel better. Here we were years later with the roles reversed. But this time we were being offered the magic answer in the form of a pill, and he just wanted me to be well again.

Ten days after starting Zoloft, I was headed home from a brunch on a Saturday afternoon. Owen was with me and we had just met up with my friends Chelsey and Corinne for a yummy breakfast at one of our favorite spots. It was a typical LA day, with the sun shining through a cloudless sky. I remember rolling to a stop sign and sighing with contentment. I'd just had a lovely morning with friends, Owen had been an angel at the restaurant, and I was headed home for a weekend with my boys. Out of nowhere I thought, "I feel happy." And when I reached the stop sign I truly stopped. I recognized happiness, and it was a blissful feeling. It had been a very long time since I truly felt that way. It was encouraging; I knew I had made the right decision seeking medical help. But my journey wasn't over.

A month after starting the medication I had a check-up with my psychiatrist. I told her that I'd definitely felt a shift in my disposition since starting the meds, but I still had disturbing thoughts that drifted in from time to time. Lows that came seemingly out of nowhere. Apathetic thoughts were the scariest. Those passive death wishes still found their way in from time to time. She decided to increase my dosage.

It helped.

I started to feel like myself again—the Meagan before giving birth. I didn't feel like a zombie or Stepford Wife version of myself, which is what I feared would happen if I started taking depression medication. Instead, I just felt like me. More balanced, more whole. I felt the gamut of normal human emotions. I still experienced sadness but I didn't feel despondent anymore. I didn't feel apathetic about my future. I didn't think life for those I loved would be unchanged if I was no longer a part of it. I felt like I had broken the water's surface and taken off my mask. I could breathe and see more clearly, without feeling like the world was slowed down and distorted.

There is a wide range of potential side effects when you take any medication. In my case, Zoloft gave me night sweats. Like soaking through my pajamas, waking up wet and uncomfortable, night sweats. I'm a big pajama pants fan but those all got tucked away for awhile. Instead I slept in oversized tees and granny panties. Super hot—literally and figuratively.

I started medication and continued seeing my therapist every other week. About two months after this routine began, I started feeling like my old self again. My therapist agreed. She said, "I think we're done. If you ever need to talk, I'll be here. But I hope not. I hope you live a happy and healthy life and you don't need to come back."

I had graduated.

Doctor's Note

Studies show that when it comes to mental health, the best results come from "multimodal treatment"; most often, a combination of psychotherapy and medication. Medication can be instrumental in addressing chemical changes, while talk therapy addresses patterns of behavior that are destructive or that ultimately add to feelings of distress.

— Abigail Levrini, Ph.D.

Chapter 22

Unconventional Move

Since February 2013, I've experienced some major life changes. I became a mother. I struggled with depression, and I finally sought help in November 2013. We've covered all of this. What I'm leaving out is that around October 2013, a month before I started my journey toward mental health, Dan and I started to seriously consider leaving LA. By August 2014, we closed on our first home . . . in Florida. We built it from the ground up.

Leaving Los Angeles, the mecca of the acting world, was not something I thought I would do unless I was ready to "give up" acting. When we made the decision to leave, I didn't feel like I was giving up, but I did know a change was needed. And sitting here, writing this book, several years after leaving LA, I know that getting help for my depression also helped me work through the enormities of building a home across the country and "leaving behind" the hustle of the acting world that had been a steady hum surrounding me since moving to NYC five days after graduating college. My therapist kept asking if I was absolutely sure I was ready to move across the country and start a new life. The answer was always, "Yes." I realized I'd been whispering "yes" for a long time internally, and I needed to finally make it a reality.

Dan and I moved to LA from New York City in January 2008, many years before Owen came into the picture. The switch was a good one. We absolutely loved LA. People scoff when they hear this. For so many, NYC is the center of the universe, the center of culture and authenticity. LA has a reputation as a shallow, glittery, lonely, stuck-in-the-car, kind of place. I'm sure that world exists, but we lucked out. We chose our apartment based on its walkability. To the north we could walk to The Grove, an outdoor shopping mall complete with it's own trolley and a Nordstrom, and to the nation's oldest Farmer's Market. To the south, we could walk to world-renowned museums like LACMA and the La Brea Tar Pits. Every place we wanted to go beyond our walking space was about a 20 minute drive, from Glendale to Santa Monica. Sure, there was traffic sometimes, but 20 minutes was the norm. Most of my castings took place within a five-mile radius of my house. Depending on how I had to dress or have my hair, I would often bike to castings if I could. I got involved with an acting studio where I met genuine, wonderful people who are still friends. And I'm not talking about a handful. I'm talking a squad that rolled 15 deep. People I'd hang out with, rehearse with, create projects with, give advice to and take advice from. I've been lucky enough to stand beside some of these people at their weddings. These friends defied expectations of what "LA people" were supposed to be like. On top of the new friends I was making, most of my nearest and dearest from NYC ended up making the same pilgrimage, and I met many of their other friends as well. My time in LA was collaborative and rich.

The weather is also a factor that cannot be underestimated. Some people don't like it when weather is consistent. They like variety and the change of seasons. While I, too, appreciate a good turn of the leaf, I did grow up in Florida so seasonal change has never been a norm for me. LA always felt like home in that way. You know, if home had zero humidity and a surprising lack of clouds and rain. LA is a weird place to be depressed because every day the weather beckons you to reconsider.

I'll always be nostalgic for LA and NYC, but for different reasons. NYC was where I spent my early 20s, making dreams into a reality and having adventures that I thought only happened to other people. I worked in commercials, films, and did some modeling, had plenty of nights out that turned into watching the sunrise, and even found true love. Life came into full color once I moved to NY, like Dorothy landing in Oz. LA, on the other hand, was where I started to become more of my own person, creating and establishing relationships beyond circumstance. I was newly married and living an adventure with my new husband in a new land, far away from our families and the worlds we'd built in our younger years. We became a true family of our own.

When we began thinking about having children, we knew we wanted to own a home instead of renting one. We began looking at real estate in LA, but grew continually frustrated. If we wanted to own a house with a yard, we'd have to look way beyond the beloved neighborhood we'd been renting in for years. In fact, to get any real value for our budget, we would have to look beyond LA proper. And when we started looking beyond LA for a place to live we started asking, "What's the point?" We were living across the country, away from our families, because of opportunities in LA. If we moved outside of LA, away from our group of friends and our magical "20 minutes to everything" location, then we might as well live, well, on the other side of the country. But we weren't quite ready to move out of California just yet, mostly because we had no idea where we'd want to move if we did.

And then Owen was born.

And everything shifted.

Priorities changed, as everyone insists they will and would. Everyone is right. It was decided. We needed to move. We wanted to be closer to family and I was done with the LA grind. I hadn't worked since the September before I got pregnant. I had sporadic auditions. I'd been hustling since 2002 and had a lot to show for it. But it wasn't enough. It wasn't where I thought I'd be, but I was tired. Tired of the casting workshops and networking and wondering when my next audition would be. I had a baby now and none of it seemed quite worth it. Meanwhile, I was struggling with depression, working overtime to maintain my normal facade. There was just too much acting. We needed a change.

But we still had no idea where that change would take us until HGTV started promoting their 2013 Smart Home Giveaway in Jacksonville Beach, FL. Their website described the home as "a high-tech, shingle-style vacation home located in the Jacksonville Beach community of Paradise Key South Beach." The look of the house was exactly what we wanted. The location of the house was everything we wanted. I quickly started entering us to win the home everyday, twice a day. I know you're reading this and thinking, "They won the house???" Sadly, no. But that giveaway gave us a starting point.

The area looked just like what we'd been picturing. I also realized that northern Florida was the perfect place to go if I wanted to pursue acting again someday. The market had totally changed since I had started working. With digital technology, many castings had moved to a self-taping system. With all of its tax incentives, Georgia had become the latest hot shooting location for shows and movies. My good friend had just booked a series regular role on a show that was based in Atlanta. Another friend was working consistently in the Southeast market. Suddenly it didn't seem like a step back to move east. It seemed like a viable way to continue working AND be closer to family. I didn't have to sacrifice one for the other anymore.

While all of this potential life-altering move-talk was happening, I realized I needed to seek help for my depression. And I did. And we know how that went. What I don't know is how advisable it is to make a major, life-changing decision while you're starting the process of therapy, but that's what I did. I think it worked for me because we had been moving toward this decision for years. We knew we wanted to be able to raise our family in a house that we owned, with a yard, with family nearby, with great schools, in a neighborhood where kids played freely. We knew that we didn't have to worry about making "the move" until our kids got closer to school age. But once we figured out where we wanted to be, it didn't seem like we should keep waiting to make it a reality.

The week of Christmas (before we headed to my parents' house for lasagna and unexpected breakdowns) we flew to Jacksonville. We had a weekend booked with a real estate agent. My brother Greg and his wife Stephanie came from Gainesville to take care of Owen while we focused on houses. We saw places that were not the right fit, we saw places that seemed dreamy but lacking, I had a meltdown in front of an aggressive sales agent in a model home (48 hours is not long enough to make a decision this huge!). Then, on our last day, on our last appointment, we found it. There was a lot in a neighborhood within walking distance of a brand-new school. The back of the lot bordered a protected preserve of woods, and the front end was on a cul-de-sac where we imagined Owen would play with his friends after school, years down the line. We could sit on our front porch and wave as he zoomed by on his bike. We went to a park to talk over everything, and Greg and Stephanie brought Owen to meet us. When they arrived, they told us to stop and watch. They let go of Owen's hands and he toddled his first steps. There's an element of magic when you see your child take their first steps. And there's magic when you find the place you're going to call home, for hopefully many, many years to come. So we toddled our first steps, too. We put a deposit down on the lot and drove down to my parents' house to celebrate the holidays. We had a lot of decisions still to make (including whether or not we wanted to back out). But the more we looked at options for house plans and the more we talked it over with family and friends, the more confident we were with our decision.

So as I rebuilt my life, we started building a home across the country.

* * * * *

The process of building a house and preparing for a huge move interestingly paralleled my treatment for depression. We found a place to call home right when I found a therapist I felt I could talk to. We were going through contracts and building plans, and picking out finishes for our dream home when I went on medication and started to feel like myself again. Perhaps it's cheesy, but building a house was not unlike rebuilding myself. It took time, and care, and detailed thought, but was ultimately so worth it.

We moved into our new home in August that year, eight months after I started medication. One of the first things I did was research psychiatrists in the area. It was going to be time to start weaning off of the medication soon and I wanted to have someone lined up to help me through the process. I also wanted to make sure I had someone to call when/if I wanted to have more children. The likelihood of experiencing postpartum depression again increases after experiencing it once. Owen was only a year-and-a-half old when we closed on our house and I wasn't quite ready to embrace the idea of having more children. But after regaining my health, I was less closed off to the idea. I told Dan, and myself, that when Owen turned two, we could start asking ourselves if we wanted another. For the next six months, however, I would enjoy our new home, our family of three, and my well-earned happiness.

Chapter 23

Two

He turned two last week, but I feel like he's been two for months now. He's taller than some three-year-olds, he can put together puzzles at a remarkable speed, and he sings along with Taylor Swift songs, filling in the blanks when I pause for the words. He is exuberant. He has the most enthusiasm of anyone I've ever known. The weight with which he shouted, "Oh No!" while watching *Big Hero 6*, as robots zoomed across the screen, narrowly missing our hero, will always stay with me. If he loses himself in play or Curious-George-watching, the need to know where I am snaps him out of it for a moment. He questions, "Mommy?" and then looks for me. When I answer, "Yes, Owen?" and he finds me, he goes back to what he's doing and says to himself, satisfied, "Yeah." I'm always nearby but he has to double-check. I look forward to his nap times, as any mama of a toddler does, if only so I can eat lunch without him climbing on me or so I can nap for a little bit, too. But if he naps for too long, I start to miss him. He runs so fast and can dribble a soccer ball better than I ever could. He never misses an opportunity to dance. There is a side table, low to the ground, in our family room that he likes to climb on top of and "stand" on his knees to perform his "ABCs." He has a great sense of humor; one of his favorite things to do is mess with us. For awhile every time we'd ask him what sound an animal made, every animal sounded like an elephant. "What sound does the cow make?" He'd blow out his elephant trunk and laugh. "What sound does the dog make" "Pmphhhhh!" He knew the answers. If someone else asked him, he'd give the right sounds. But if it was his dad or me, "Pmphhhh!" accompanied with an all-knowing grin.

We're trying for another baby. Right after Owen was born, I thought I'd made the biggest mistake of my life. Once I started to adjust, I thought he'd be an only child. Eventually I thought we could start discussing the possibility of more children once he turned two. And now I can't wait to get pregnant. My only point of anxiety is, "How will I ever love another child as much as I love Owen?" It's a genuine worry that I'm sure all parents-of-one think. Sorry, Future Child. While I know this is a common worry, somehow I think that next kid comes along and you just break open again and the love grows.

I'm not worried about having postpartum depression again. Statistics indicate that I have a higher risk of experiencing it again, since I had it the first go-round. And it could happen. But now I know better. My husband knows better. My family knows better. My friends know better. We know how it can look, and how it can be masked, and we're going to be more watchful. I can choose to go back on Zoloft right after giving birth. If the depression seeps back in, I wouldn't have to wait as long for the medication to take effect and feel better. I can go on medication before giving birth. I can just wait and see how I feel. I haven't decided the best path for me yet, but I have a great psychiatrist who knows my history. And I'm not afraid of medication anymore. I know how much it can help, if I need it. I'm most looking forward to experiencing my next child's early life how I wish I had been able to experience Owen's: healthily.

But that whole love thing? That whole thing that I was worried about not feeling the first instant I saw Owen? I shouldn't have been worried. It came. It was built. In moments, in touches, in looks, in heart against heart, in tears, in sighs. I fell in love. In that crazy, tidal-wave-flood-of-love way I had hoped for. And there is no going back.

I am his mom.

And he is my heart.

And I'm ready to make room for more.

Part Two:

On Miscarriage & Fertility

Chapter 24

Seeing Double

I posted an excerpt from this book on my blog for the first time on May 8, 2015. On May 9th I took a pregnancy test.

Positive.

I was tentatively excited. We started trying in January and each month led only to single lines on the tests. I was supposed to get my period on May 8th so I took an early-detection test two days earlier. It showed that same single line. So when my period didn't show up on the 8th, I was surprised. We had a wedding to go to on the night of the 9th. I thought that I better take another test just to be sure I could indulge in the champagne toast. That double line told me to abstain.

This pregnancy hit hard. I already had my psychiatrist at the ready if my moods started to feel wonky, but I didn't feel any of the familiar depression symptoms yet. And I wasn't letting myself think too far ahead. Instead I just felt the normal making-a-human-is-hard-work-*tired.* Times ten. Like unreasonably exhausted. Forget waking up at five am to get some writing done. I had to sleep. Forget doing any sort of housework while Owen napped. I needed to nap, too. I was dragging myself through the days. And I was ravenous. I never got back to my pre-pregnancy weight after Owen was born. I was still nearly fifteen pounds heavier than those pre-baby days. My clothes didn't fit properly and now they weren't going to for at least another year so I threw my eating habits to the wind and indulged my cravings. Not that I was having any particularly specific cravings. I was just craving *more.* More bread, more sugar, more hibernating foods. "Fatten me up real good," my body seemed to say.

I wasn't shy about this pregnancy. With Owen we held the news as a closely guarded secret until after the first trimester. This time we threw that caution out the window. We've been pregnant before! No problems! Why not celebrate all the way through this time around?

My best friend was the first person I told. She was watching Owen while we went to the wedding that night, so I thought it'd be fun to tell her even though we had just found out that morning. She was also tentatively excited for us. We told our families the next day. Everyone was tentatively excited too. They wanted to know who they could tell, and we said, "Anyone you want!" Though we added, "As long as you'd be comfortable telling them if something goes wrong." But we all dismissed that caveat as superstition.

I told my mama friend, K., later that week. She knew we'd been trying since the beginning of the year. She has a son a few weeks younger than Owen, and she also had a tough time after he was born. She wasn't quite ready to add to her brood yet, but she was excited that we were ready. I texted her a picture of the pregnancy test. She texted back all the appropriate emojis and then sent a picture of her own. She was pregnant, too! Surprise! Like *for real* surprise. Ready or not, here baby comes. At least we had each other to navigate this second pregnancy. We knew each other's history and struggles, so we knew that having someone else to go through everything with is invaluable. I told my neighbor. I told my son's teacher on his last day of school. He was playing with a baby doll during the end-of-school party. She mentioned how nurturing he is with baby dolls. "Do you want to have more children?" Well, since you asked, "Yes. I actually just found out I'm pregnant. It's still very new, but we're excited." She was excited, too. She said Owen would be a great big brother.

My childhood best friends were in town over Memorial Day, so we hosted a barbecue at our house to catch up. The mother of one of my friends joined as well. Her first words when she saw me were, "I see we're expecting another!" I could have burst into tears, considering I was only about five weeks along. How could she tell? Were those hibernating-eating-habits already showing? Or is it because I never lost all the weight from Owen? Or is she just a witchy-woman with a sense for this sort of thing? Instead of crying, I just confirmed. These were my oldest friends so why not share the news? So even though it was new news, everyone at the BBQ found out.

I called to set up a doctor's appointment and was surprised to hear they would see me as early as seven weeks. "The earlier, the better," I thought. My fellow pregnant friend, K., was surprised as well. Her doctor wanted to wait until the nine-week-mark. We texted back and forth. "How are you feeling today?" she'd ask. "Exhausted," I'd answer. "How about you?" "Sick," she'd say. I had the blahs and she had the blechs. One Friday I couldn't get off the couch. My stomach felt unsettled, like I might be sick, but I never actually vomited. I turned on the TV and Owen was in heaven. Mommy doesn't feel good but that means TV! PBS Kids got us through that day. Thankfully, I started to feel a little more balanced over the weekend. And a little less tired. It was nice to have a break from feeling so unwell.

My first doctor's appointment came quickly. My neighbor's daughter watched Owen. She didn't know what the appointment was for, but I told my neighbor I'd show her daughter the ultrasound when we got home if we had good news.

* * * * *

Seeing Spots

I told Dan I was nervous.

"Why are you nervous?" he asked.

I said, "Imagine I told you that you were pregnant. Would you believe it? Being a man has nothing to do with it," I tried to explain. "Sure, I feel tired and run down and super hungry. But otherwise, I still feel like me. I can't be sure there's a baby growing inside of me until I see it on the ultrasound. It would be the same if I told you, 'You have a human growing inside of you.' You wouldn't believe me until you saw proof. And I want this baby to be proven." He seemed to get it.

This was the first time I had seen this doctor. The waiting room was a zoo. There were so many visibly pregnant women. It was a little overwhelming. It seemed like there was a population explosion going on in our neck of the woods. So we waited. And waited. And waited to be seen. Dan's patience was running thin. He had blocked out a couple of hours for the appointment but he had a meeting that he'd soon be late for. Finally, they called us back to the exam room.

Because it was still early in the pregnancy, the doctor reminded me that it would be too soon to hear a heartbeat. But with an intravaginal ultrasound, they could measure the baby and make sure everything was on track. She poked around my uterus until the darkness revealed a little spot in the sea of open space in my womb. A spot. Not a baby. Her brow furrowed. "Hmmm . . . are you sure about the date of your last period?" she asked. "Yes," I answered. "Very sure. Why?" I asked, even though I knew the answer. Something wasn't right.

She said we were looking at an egg sac smaller than what the baby should be at this point. But this happens, she assured us. Sometimes the conception date is off. She wanted to set up an appointment for the following week to measure again. I wanted further clarification.

"What does it mean if there isn't really any growth next week?" I asked. She answered that it would be considered a missed miscarriage. 'Missed' because I wasn't exhibiting any symptoms such as cramps or bleeding.

She didn't print any pictures to take home with us.

And there it was.

All the caveats. And tentativeness. And tempered hope. All there in a dot.

Not a baby.

There was another couple in line behind us when we were setting up our appointment for the next week. They had their daughter, who seemed a little older than Owen, with them. The little girl told us proudly, "I'm going to be a big sister!" Her mom laughed and it was clear that it was early on in her pregnancy, too. I forced back tears. I had already ordered a shirt for Owen that said, "Rad Big

Bro." We had already started taking weekly pictures of my pregnancy. Six weeks. Seven weeks. Dot dot dot.

I let go of my tears when we got in the car, but I still held onto hope. It was possible that I ovulated later than we thought. My last period had arrived five days earlier than scheduled. It was weird when it showed up on a Monday instead of a Friday. So if I had ovulated based on the Friday schedule, I *would* be measuring about a week smaller. We clung tightly to that idea while we waited for the week to go by. It was a week full of anxiety and hope and dread and "what-if." Stress wasn't going to help anything, so we put on our happy faces. But next week's ultrasound was knocking around my mind constantly. And I wasn't feeling sick anymore.

We told our families. We told our friends. I told my neighbor. "The baby is measuring smaller than she should be," we said, "but we won't know for sure why until next week. We'll keep you posted." And yes, Dan and I both felt this baby was a she. We were pretty excited to have a little girl.

The next week came and the fragile hope we walked in with crumbled quickly when we saw our dot on the screen. The doctor had a saddened tone. "Unfortunately, it's measuring the same as last week and you can see here where the egg sac is starting to break loose from the uterine lining. I'm sorry," she said. I knew though. The night before our second appointment I had a wave of menstrual cramps. It lasted all of a minute but it was distinct. Then I went to the bathroom and when I wiped there was a faint pink smear. I thought, "Well, I better put on a pad because I'm about to have a miscarriage." Then . . . nothing. I didn't bleed anymore. Was it possible I was just spotting? Spotting can be a normal symptom of pregnancy. Were the cramps also normal? I had heard that they could be. This fragile hope was a facade to get me through the night and the hours before the appointment the next day.

But I knew the baby was not there anymore. I wanted to believe that my instincts were wrong so I let myself, but mother's intuition is rarely wrong. *That* I believe wholeheartedly.

And so at the 8-week appointment we were given our options:

1. I could wait for my body to miscarry on it's own.

2. I could take medication to speed up the process.

3. I could have a procedure.

I didn't have to decide yet. I could go home and think about it. If I decided to use medication, they could call it into my pharmacy. If I decided to have surgery, they could schedule the procedure at the hospital.

In the meantime, I could wait.

Chapter 25

My Choices

We were running into a timing problem. It was Wednesday. My in-laws and my two teenage nieces were scheduled to arrive for a week-long visit on Saturday. The following Thursday we were leaving for Colorado to visit friends. The next two weeks were packed with plans. I didn't want to wait around for my body to get the memo that it was time to let go of the baby. I didn't know what to do. I didn't want to do anything. But sitting around waiting for a miscarriage to happen didn't seem like an option.

I texted my mom after the appointment. I said, "Not good news." I knew she was at work but I also knew she was waiting to hear from me. She called back immediately. I cried. I told her my options. She said whatever I decided, she would drive up, even if it was just for a hug. I cried more. It was in that moment that I knew I had made the right decision to move back east. It meant the world that my mom was able to come when I needed her most. I told her I'd let her know what I decided.

I decided to take the medicine to induce the miscarriage. I didn't want to let this miscarriage ruin my plans more than it already had. Trying to keep a semblance of normalcy felt like the right decision in this very abnormal time.

Dan picked up the prescription, along with some pads. I googled "what to expect when using medication for a miscarriage." I didn't find much but I did find one blog that was really helpful and generous with details. I felt like I had a better idea of what the next few days would be like. I had to insert the pills vaginally. It would take a few hours to start working, but I'd start to feel some bad cramping and then I'd have heavy, chunky bleeding that would taper off to more regular bleeding, like a menstrual flow. Sounded like a real blast. I hoped I'd be able to sleep through most of it.

My mom was going to arrive around noon so I went ahead and did my first dose at 10am. I'd have to do the second dose twelve hours later. By the time she got in, I would be starting to experience symptoms. I could hole myself up in my room while she watched Owen. And that's what I did. I started to feel some mild cramping so I went ahead and popped some Tylenol and went to bed once she arrived.

And I waited.

I woke up and checked my pad. Nothing.

I kept waiting.

We ate dinner and there was a huge rainbow over the house as we finished up. Owen ran out to see it. It was still raining lightly. He reached his hand out beyond the eave of the porch to touch the rain. I snapped a photo and it looks like he's trying to touch the rainbow. A baby conceived after a miscarriage is known as a "rainbow baby." The timing of the rainbow over our house was not lost on any of us. Dan said it was our baby letting us know she was ok and that she'd be back when the time was right. It was a nice thought.

I kept waiting.

But there wasn't any bleeding. There was nothing.

The next day I didn't know what to do because the medicine was clearly not working. I called the doctor, who said that it can take up to 48 hours to see results. She said if the weekend passed and nothing had changed to call them back. This was news to me. I didn't realize that the medicine could take so long to work, or that it might not work at all. Awesome.

My mom and I decided to go to the mall to pass the time. Maybe being up and walking around would speed things up. I was essentially waiting for labor, after all. I continued having mild cramps, but not bleeding. I popped some more Tylenol and kept waiting.

And waiting.

And waiting.

Friday turned into Saturday, the day my in-laws and nieces were arriving. My mom waited until our company arrived before heading back to her house. It had been 48 hours since I had taken the medicine and it didn't look like it was going to be effective.

My body does not like getting rid of babies.

With Owen, my water broke but I never went into labor on my own. I had to be induced. There were never any true signs that I was having a miscarriage and the medicine used to induce wasn't even working. It felt cruel.

I called my doctor on Monday and told them that the medicine had not worked, and that I wanted to go ahead and have the surgery. At this point I was angry with my body. I just wanted this all over with. They could get me in the next day.

I sat my nieces down that night. I told them that I was excited for them to visit because I was excited to be able to tell them in person that they were going to be getting another cousin. But I had lost the baby. And I had to go have a procedure done as a result, so I wouldn't be around the next day. And they were pretty amazing.

They didn't say much or offer any platitudes. They just hugged me for a really long time. It was exactly what I needed.

I wore my Superman shirt the next day to the hospital. Sometimes it's the little things that help you feel strong. I filled out paperwork and the doctor came in and introduced himself and explained the procedure. The anesthesiologist came by as well to explain how he was going to put me completely under.

I had to fill out more paperwork once I was being prepped for surgery; one particular form was a doozy. Florida law requires you to specify what should be done with the "fetal remains" if you're having a dilation and curettage (a D&C) at 20 weeks or less. Did I want the hospital to dispose of them? Did I want them transferred to a funeral home? Being that my miscarriage was so early on, this was an unexpected detail to think about. My heart broke for the person who had fought for this law to be put in place. The law was named for a specific person and I can just imagine their grieving process when the hospital hadn't given them the option of a funeral. The form itself was unpleasant—the term "fetal remains" is hard to face—but I understood why it was needed. It made me even sadder.

They wheeled me back and it reminded me of my c-section. Suddenly, I was alone in a cold room with only medical staff around. The vibe here was a very different vibe though because there were only men on the medical staff. In LA all of the doctors and nurses were women in the operating room. They gave me a drug to make me pass out and I remember the doctor asking how I was feeling. Admittedly, I felt good. "Feels like college," I responded. I heard everyone laugh as I went to sleep.

Then it was over.

When I was in recovery, one of the nurses asked how I was feeling. "Ok, I guess," was my response. Then she said something about being sorry and asked if I was trying to get pregnant. I nodded and started to cry again. And she apologized again. Since that incident I've totally regretted that I was groggy from the anesthesia because I wish I could have shouted, "What the fuck does it matter? And how the fuck is it any of your business? And fuckity fuck fuck

fuck!" I am not one who curses with abandon. Or at all really. But I feel like a few 'fucks' were called for in that particular situation. When a woman has a D&C, you shouldn't ask if she was *trying* for the baby that she just lost. Because it doesn't matter. A baby has been lost.

And then came the healing.

The rest of the day I was a little unsteady. The anesthesia made my legs feel like a young colt's. My neighbor stopped by to see me. Owen played with his grandparents and cousins. And I was glad that it was over. I felt like I could start healing. And then I felt lucky that the timing was what it was. I didn't have time to sit around and feel sorry for myself. The next day we drove to Gainesville so my nieces could tour the University of Florida. My older niece had just finished her freshman year in high school and was very interested in their nursing program. So I got to see my brother and sister-in-law the day after surgery. Being surrounded by the people I love is something that I don't take for granted, especially since I didn't have that physical proximity to family for the past decade. I missed my sister and know she wished she was closer. She sent a lovely gift basket of bath products and a playlist of songs so that I could unwind and relax. Music is therapeutic for both of us; only she could have come up with the right mix.

The rest of the week was full of the busy-ness of out of town guests and then Saturday arrived, the day of my annual Waffle Party, aka, my birthday party. I could have decided not to do it. I could have told everyone I wasn't feeling well and canceled. But I wanted to be distracted and surrounded by friends and family.

About twenty neighbors and friends came over for homemade waffles and coffee and it was all going great until Owen looked out the window and started shouting, "It's a baby!! A baby!!" and then ran to get the door. One of my neighbors had just given birth to her new baby three weeks before, right when I found out that I wasn't going to be having my baby. I was actually really glad that she was able to come, but my friends who knew about the miscarriage were nervous. Was I going to be OK seeing a newborn baby? Was I going to be OK seeing how excited Owen was? Was I going to be OK holding the baby? The answer was yes to all of it.

For some reason it felt comforting to hold this baby. Maybe because

I knew that my neighbor had fertility issues and had her own trying

journey to bring her baby into the world. Maybe it gave me a little

hope? Maybe because that new-baby smell and the feel of new baby

skin is chemically engineered by evolution to bring a sense of peace?

I don't know exactly why I was OK with it, but I was. I was very OK

in the moment. I held her sweet baby boy and breathed in the smell

of hope. Because in that moment, I hoped that I'd have another

chance. A chance to get pregnant again. A chance to have another

baby of my own to hold. A chance to care for that baby when I'm of

healthy mind.

Everyone, including my doctors, said that the rate of

conception immediately after a miscarriage is much higher. For some

reason people get pregnant quickly if they want to. But I wasn't quite

ready to think about that yet. Even though I had hope at my birthday

party, it was more of a distant hope that one day I would be ready to

take that chance again.

That night I had to get out of the house. We went to dinner and I had a good cry—a body-heaving, heart-heavy, cathartic cry. The next week we went to Colorado and had some healing time with close friends, as our babies played together in the fresh mountain air. When we got back from that trip, Dan and my best friend Kristen did a three-day juice cleanse with me. I felt like I literally needed to reset my body. I lost those few extra pounds I gained while I was pregnant and I saw clearly the unhealthy eating habits I had developed. I started to make changes. Dan and I started running again, and I started to feel healthier. And lighter. Both physically and metaphysically.

Chapter 26

Tossing Stones

I'm still healing, in a way. I've accepted this miscarriage and grieved for it and am changed from it. After the D&C, my doctor recommended I wait two menstrual cycles before trying for another baby. That way the uterine lining would have a chance to rebuild which could lower my chances of another miscarriage. It felt like a relief to have a medical reason to wait before trying again. Since my doctors and friends told me I could "get pregnant right away" after a miscarriage, I felt like there was pressure to hurry up and get pregnant or I would miss my window. I wasn't ready for it yet. But give me a few months? Maybe I'd be ready then. My first period didn't show up until seven weeks after the surgery. And the next one came a little sooner than the normal 28-day cycle. My body is still trying to find its equilibrium, which feels . . . right. We were knocked off balance and my footing is still unsure. Everyone's healing process is different. I might get pregnant again, or I might not. I might get pregnant and lose another baby. That's the reality that I don't think I quite grasped before I miscarried. I see now that in so many ways I was incredibly lucky with Owen. We had an easy time conceiving and I had a healthy pregnancy. I took it for granted in ways I didn't realize. I get it now. And the more I talk with women I know, the more I find out that they have had similar struggles. But I never knew because miscarriage is not something we talk about openly. It took me a little while to start talking as well. But now I'm talking. And I hope you will, too.

If I've learned anything from my struggles with PPD, and now with fertility, it's that there is comfort and grace in knowing I am not alone. As I've opened myself up, others have opened themselves to me. And it's been a tonic to my soul.

Truly.

So *thank you.*

Thank you for being brave and sharing your voice. And your time. And your support just from reading along. We never know how far the ripples of our stone will stretch when we toss it in the water. But we know that our load is lighter without that extra stone in our pocket.

Part Three:

Not Alone

Chapter 27

Her Story, Your Story

After working on this book for a few months, I knew that I wanted to include the stories of women in my life who have experienced struggles after having their children, too. Their stories are a little different from mine because they were not diagnosed with clinical postpartum depression like I was, but they faced difficulties that made me realize I wasn't alone in my challenges. If you've picked up this book and gotten this far, chances are you or someone you know well, has similar struggles. We put on a mask of normalcy to help get through the day and oftentimes it's accepted as truth. I wish I had been more vulnerable to my truth. The truth that I was not ok, that I wasn't sure how I would make it through each day. That I didn't love motherhood as much as I always thought I would. That I just wanted to get away. That I wanted to be gone. But that feeling of "not loving motherhood" feels so shameful. I felt so guilty. It feels like such a betrayal to the tiny human that you love, even if you don't love all the changes that come along with him. Becoming a mother can feel like a complete upheaval of your existence. Some women find that a welcome change. The "focusing on someone other than myself is such a relief" trope is often tossed about. You don't often hear about how difficult it can be to suddenly not have time or energy for yourself. Sometimes just getting to the bathroom is a struggle. Nearly three years later, I still wonder when I'll be able to poop in peace again. The other day, Owen threw himself at my feet, sobbing, while I went to the bathroom because, "I want to poop toooooooo". "You have to wait your turn. Mommy is pooping now."

Really.

Basic human functions are no longer your own. In the beginning, I waited until he was sleeping before using the bathroom. What if the moment I sat down, he needed me? And, yes, I have used the bathroom while holding him. That makes wiping an adventure. Excuse all the potty talk. Or should I say, "Potty Talk! Your Main Source of Conversation as a Parent!"

The bottom (hehe) line is that the more we talk openly about the various adjustments that occur when a baby comes into our lives, the broader a sense of community we will have. And knowing that you're not alone in how you're adjusting (or not adjusting) to your new role can make all the difference in getting through the days. It can make you feel OK that some days you just want to scream (because trust me, we've all been there).

I gave each of the contributors the same list of questions, and each had the option of being interviewed by me directly with these questions as prompts or using them to brainstorm and write their own stories. What follows is a beautiful mix of interviews, personal essays, and conversations. I love that the structures of their stories are as unique as the mothers who share them. Maybe you'll see pieces of your own story reflected in theirs.

Chapter 28

Jes's Story

"I didn't want anyone to know I was having such a hard time"

"I wish someone would have just told me . . ." She pauses to collect herself as she chokes back tears. "Like how hard it was going to be, you know? And how lonely it was going to be. You think that you have a baby and you're like, 'I'm not going to be lonely. I have someone to be with me.' I don't think anyone tells you how hard it's going to be. And I'm not quite sure why."

* * * * *

My interview with Jes got *real* real, *real* quickly. Just two minutes into our conversation and we were both crying, remembering those early days of motherhood. This wasn't surprising, given the way we cut through the bullshit when we first met, when her baby was a fresh six-weeks-old and Owen was only eight weeks. Standing in her kitchen, relating immediately about our troubles with breastfeeding was something we both needed at that time. Being able to share our early-day woes with one another made a big difference in both of our lives. During that first year we had each other to text or call or just sit with in a park and that was invaluable. But Jes's journey was different than mine. In addition to being thrust into motherhood, she also juggled her bartending job and going back to college. She was a full-time student studying bio-science and chemistry when she had her daughter. She's going to save the world, y'all.

When we did this interview, we hadn't spoken on the phone in the nearly two years since I had left LA. We'd texted and kept up with each other through pictures and social media but life is busy and time-zone differences can be hard to navigate. Even though so much time had passed, we picked up right where we left off. We didn't skip a beat. Below is a bit of our hour-long conversation.

* * * * *

Me: *So what was your biggest struggle as a new mom?*

Jes: Breastfeeding, for sure. For sure, for sure. I didn't get a lot of milk and just going back to work so fast, it was difficult to pump. And she wasn't a good eater or latch-er-on-er. And I was hell-bent on not doing formula. So that was a huge struggle.

Me: *Did it ever get easier? Or did you decide to go for formula?*

Jes: It got easier for a little bit. We kind of got into a nice rhythm. And her and I kind of figured each other out. But then it was three times that I got mastitis. And it just hurt so bad. And I had to come home from work and pump and it would hurt. And I think I was just frustrated. And it was actually at a play center where I was talking to a lady and I think she just saw my struggle and she said, "It should be like a dance. And if you're not feeling it or they're not feeling it, it's ok to just stop. I know society says blahblahblah," Like some random lady! And like a week later I stopped. And I told my husband, "She's right. I'm not enjoying this." That was like six months, I think? I wish I had gone longer, but I don't know. I was just done.

Me: *I made it nine weeks before I said, "Nope! Done!"*

Jes: And I'm out!

Me: *So if that was your biggest struggle, what came the most naturally for you?*

Jes: Probably calming her down. And soothing her, I guess. I think at first I tried to soothe her with my boob, obviously, but then I figured out different ways to do that. I don't think I ever had a time where I was wanting to pull my hair out and didn't like her. Do you know what I mean? And I don't know. I mean, I had a lot of signs of postpartum but I didn't have the one where you feel detached from your child.

Me: *What do you wish you had known before you gave birth?*

Jes: I think what I said earlier. Just that it's going to be really effing hard! And your hormones are going to be all over the place. And you're going to be sad and you're going to be happy and you might sit on the bathroom floor and cry for no apparent reason and that that's ok. And that it's ok to maybe stop breastfeeding. And it's ok to not have the most expensive diapers. I just wish everybody didn't just glorify it and make it look like it was so zen. Because then you're like, "What am *I* doing wrong?" Because it's not so easy. Sometimes I wish the moms at the park would just drop it. And be like, "Yeah this is hard! I'm having a hard time too!" I think so many of us just try to hold up this like, "I'm doing the best and I'm doing great" but we're really not. It would be great if we just told each other that we're not.

Me: *If you could have a conversation with your pre-mom self, what piece of advice would you give?*

Jes: I would for sure, for sure, one hundred percent say, "Put down the dishrag. Stop folding the laundry. Stop worrying about how clean your house is and **enjoy your baby**." And, "Sleep when they sleep!" I think I was trying to uphold that [perfect mom] image in my head and I would try to keep our house clean instead of just laying there. I mean, I did lay with her a lot. But I wish, now that she's getting bigger, I think, "I wish I had put down the damn dishtowel and just laid with her or stared at her or touched her." You know?

Me: *If you went back to work, what was the hardest adjustment?*

Jes: Definitely lack of sleep. Especially trying to go back to school that same following semester was really difficult. I think it was just difficult to balance everything. And I was pumping downstairs [at work] in the nasty bathroom and I felt like a cow. I think that after going back to work, on top of being back at school, on top of taking care of her, I don't think I had enough time for myself. And I think that I definitely had postpartum [depression], I think there's still a part of me that has that lingering. And I think that if I wouldn't have had to go back to work or done school or chosen both, I think I would of had time for myself and taken care of myself. I don't think I even knew what was wrong with me! I just kept going through the motions because I was so busy. I had to finish this for school and I had to be here for work and I don't think I had the time to realize like how sad and messed up I was in my head. And like, as she's gotten older and the load gets a little bit less, I find a little bit of who I was and who I love creeps out a little bit everyday. So it's like I'm starting to find myself again. And love myself again. Where I think before I didn't have the time and I wish that I would have right away. I think that if maybe I would have done that, it would have been better for me and better for her. And better for Mike. Maybe better for our marriage? I don't know.

Me: *What was the best thing about going back to work? And to school?*

Jes: Getting time to myself. It sounds so bad. Getting time to myself and with work, being able to interact with adults instead of being home. On the sad side, I was busy but on the plus side, it got me out. Just because I was a bartender and everybody wants to know about your baby and you're excited and expressing excitement. But it's so weird because I would be there and so excited and then I would leave and still be so sad. It was so confusing.

Me: *So you've kind of touched on my last question, which is did you experience postpartum depression and/or anxiety? Because I kind of think of them as the same. They're two sides of a coin.*

Jes: Yeah, I totally feel that I did. I was tested for it. It was a short brief exam for postpartum but nothing that really gave me any information or a follow-up. The weird thing was that I had all the signs of postpartum except that I wasn't detaching myself from my daughter. But still, everything that had to do with me, for sure.

And I still, I don't know if it was P. or my situation with Mike but I . . . I probably stopped about a year ago but I used to cry in the shower every day, every other day. And doubt! Wondering if I was doing it right and didn't know if I was screwing her up. Just that constant beating yourself up and self-doubt instead of self-love, you know? And I think there's a lot of elements that go along with it because I think I also wonder if I had been at home, like near my sister or my mom or somebody that could have maybe recognized what was happening or helped me or talked me through. I mean, I had you guys. Which was, like you and Heather, you guys are probably the only reason I made it through that first year. And I told my mom that. I couldn't have made it without you guys.

Me: *I wrote that in the book. I feel like the exact same way.*

Jes: Yeah, like no way in hell. Like I feel like we were all placed in each other's life and we were all soooo different....

Me: *Yes!*

Jes: But we shared with each other our differences and we still related with how hard things were and we pushed each other to be better and it was ok if we weren't. And it was just a good [thing], I am so glad that I had you guys. I wouldn't have made it without it. I really wouldn't have.

I think that it's a weird . . . I definitely think postpartum is something that needs to be paid more attention to. So I'm glad that you're writing this and I'm glad that you're getting different perspectives because not everyone's story is the same but it's all the same sadness and anxiety and like self-doubt. And even just being lost and detached from everybody. I was never lost and detached from P. but I definitely was from everybody else. Maybe not you and Heather because it was a good relationship but definitely Mike. Definitely my mom. Definitely my friends, for sure. And that's weird. And lonely. I think postpartum is very lonely.

I'm, like, sitting in a park, crying.

Me: *I know! I'm sorry!*

Jes: No, I love it. I'm glad. It helps to talk about it. I'm just glad you're bringing it to people's attention.

Me: *Thank you.*

Jes: Actually, here's a question for you. If someone were to tell you all the awful things that might happen, would you still want to have kids? Sometimes I wonder if maybe that's why no one tells you.

Me: *I feel like if someone had told me, I wouldn't believe them. Because I would think it would be different for me. You know? Like I can handle it.*

Jes: Yeah, like no big deal.

Me: *Yeah like, "I'm sorry you had a rough time but I got this." I think that was always my naïveté. And my hubris. You know just over-confidence of imagining how it was all going to be and know that I could handle everything.*

Jes: Well you kind of did! You baked cakes at like 9am, you fucker.

Me: *Well, see that was part of my coping.*

Jes: You were like, "Come over to my house," and you're like, "Oh yeah, I baked a cake" And I'm like, "I haven't even combed my hair!"

Me: *Yeah but see that was how I coped, right? Like for me, I had to stay busy and I wrote in the book . . . actually it's set up, I have a chapter called 'Jes and Heather' and I talk about you guys and then the chapter after that is 'Keeping Busy' and how I didn't allow myself downtime because if I did, then I'd have to think about how unhappy I was.*

Jes: Totally.

Me: *Or not even how unhappy but how unfeeling I was. That I was just going through motions and how I was supposed to be experiencing all this joy and love and I wasn't. You know?*

Jes: Totally. I think my school did that. My school and work just kept me so busy. And you know what's funny? Now that you say that because you say, if you were to stop, you would realize how non-feeling you were? I think that's why I cried in the shower. Because that was my time to stop. Wow. Crazy. I never thought about that. I always was like, "Why do you cry in the shower?" I know that was like a private place but I think it was where I had a moment to stop and my reality was like, "Whoa." Sometimes I feel like I wasn't even there.

Me: *Yeah. Yeah! Absolutely.*

Jes: Which is a weird . . . I don't know. I look at how I would not sleep and wake up and feed her and I wasn't even there. Wasn't there mentally. Not for myself, not for Mike. Just everything for her.

I think that's why I'm scared to have another child. It was tough. But I feel like maybe now that I'm aware of those things, I feel like maybe I have an idea of what it might be. I mean, every child is going to be different but you have an idea of what the loneliness might be. Or how to be aware of it and acknowledge it.

Have you been finding that postpartum is more prevalent with the first child or does it get worse with your second child?

Me: *As far as research goes, if you've experienced postpartum depression, you are more likely to experience it again but some people are fine with their first child and it's with their second child they get postpartum or their third or their fourth. It doesn't happen until later. And I think that one of the most common threads I'm finding is that **we don't know what we're experiencing**. I was just talking to a mom today in the park and postpartum depression came up and my book came up and I was saying that I didn't seek treatment until Owen was almost ten months old because I didn't know what was wrong with me. I just thought this was my new reality. And she said, "Oh my god, me too." And she had a very* *different experience but it was when her baby was ten-months-old that she finally sought help. It's like that weird ten-month mark for some reason I've found with a couple people. And that's just my own talking to people, not any sort of clinical research. It can happen any time between pregnancy and up to twelve months. So you can be fine for say the first six months and then all the sudden start experiencing postpartum depression. Or you could start experiencing it while you're pregnant and not realize what it is.*

Jes: Wow, that's crazy.

Me: *And I think that it just happens . . . you know, they say 1 out of 4 pregnancies or whatever you could experience PPD. I mean, the statistics are wildly varying and that's just what the statistics say. You know, "8-12% or 1 out of 4", you know?*

Jes: And you're like, What? Did you just use that in the same sentence?

Me: *Exactly, so it's interesting to me because I think it just happens so much more often because I don't think it's so often that we actually seek treatment.*

Jes: I was going to say—this is outlandish to say—but I feel like there's got be some level of postpartum issues for every woman. Like with the surge of your hormones. Or, I don't know, maybe some experience it a little bit and some experience it a lot. And I just feel like to not experience it at all is weird. How did they diagnose it? Like if everyone were to go seek treatment, or if everyone that had a baby had to have some sort of class or education on what are the signs or symptoms are? Or if was just more talked about?

Me: *There's actually a government task force this past year that recommended mandatory screenings for every woman at like 6 weeks postpartum.*

Jes: Ok, that's amazing.

Me: *And I do think that's amazing also. A friend of mine that just had a baby in January. Her pediatrician gave her a questionnaire at her daughter's, I think, 2 week check up? It was either her two-week or six-week check up and they were like, "You need to call your primary care." It was one of those things where she hadn't been asked the questions. And when you're asked the* *questions and you start to think about it, you start to realize there's something wrong. I mean, if I had been asked . . . I remember clearly, my ob-gyn asked me at my six week [checkup], "Are you ok? Have you been crying a lot?" And, "Yeah, well, I'm crying a lot but I think that's pretty normal" is how I answered. And that was it. That was the end of the conversation. Like I think if there was an actual questionnaire that asked you pointed questions about I think sleep habits, I think mental state, you know all the different things that contribute to it, we would get a lot more diagnoses.*

Jes: I think that would be a good place to do it too, like where you go for your 2-week and your 6-week because then it's consistent for you. I think what you said about "you just thought this was my reality?" Like I think that's what everybody thinks. That's definitely what I thought. I thought, "I guess this is my new life. I don't sleep, I'm super sad, and this is my reality." And if someone had asked me at 2 weeks or 4 weeks or 6 weeks, you have to ask yourself, kind of out loud . . . that's crazy to think about.

Me: *And the thing is, it looks different on everyone. Even if we're experiencing the same things. And that's the same with just 'standard' depression. I don't know how to put it. Just every depressed person, you think they're going to be sad or they're going to be irritable. But there's the happy depressives. There's the Robin Williams of the world. Where they're putting on a show but in private it's a very different story. Depression doesn't always look like how you think it should look like.*

Jes: Exactly.

Me: *And that was one of the things my first therapist I spoke to in LA said, was that she said one of the first things she asks her patients is, "Are you crying a lot?" And if they say yes, she says, "Great. You're not depressed." Because depression is the absence of emotions. Because they are depressed. The things you're supposed to experience are no longer there. I think just even having that awareness. Like I had NO CLUE. I thought that if I was depressed I would be sad all the time, right? But instead I was just bitter and angry and just unfeeling about most things.*

Jes: Even about O too, right?

Me: *Yeah, he was always great. And he was just a great baby. I got incredibly lucky with him. There was nothing wrong with him. I think that's not always the case for women. Sometimes they experience a colicky baby and that feeds into things more. But if you were to look at him as a baby, you wouldn't think I had a reason to be upset. That was the other thing. And I wasn't necessarily upset, I just didn't feel the joy that I thought was going to come with motherhood. I loved him. I didn't ever want to hurt him. I didn't feel unattached to him. I always cared if he cried or I always wanted to take care of him. And it wasn't until I went on medication that I realized I wasn't happy. Because I started to feel happy again and I was like, "Oh my god. I feel happy. I haven't felt this."*

Jes: I remember that.

Me: *It was a very weird experience, as a person who has always been happy in her life.*

Jes: Totally. To not be happy and wonder.

Me: *And everybody tells you, Oh you're going to experience baby blues....*

Jes: The baby blues? Oh great. Can you be a little more specific?

Me: *Yeah, and if it lasts longer than two weeks maybe you should be concerned. But I was exhausted. I was recovering from a c-section.*

Jes: Yeah, everything takes like eons . . .

Me: *Yeah, everything was going to take a long time.*

Jes: Also like, with postpartum maybe from a scientific perspective or a research perspective, there's so many factors. Like you said, have a caesarean, don't have a caesarean. Have a colicky baby, don't have a colicky baby. Have good eating habits, don't have good eating habits. I just feel like there's so many factors involved. And I just wish our society would look into it or pay more attention to it because there are so many factors. Like you said, depression is different on every person.

Me: *Yeah, and there's also, you kind of touched on it, I think the support system is a big factor.*

Jes: Definitely, yeah.

Me: *So if you're like us and you didn't have any family around, and we were lucky to find each other, you know and have mom friends. But we were also dealing with our own children so it's not like we could be there just to hold the baby. You know? We had to hold our own babies as well. Just moments like that. There was someone that was like, Yeah my mom comes over so I can take a shower and just hold the baby for like fifteen minutes.*

Jes: Ha!

Me: *Yeah! I'm like, Excuse me? People do that?*

Jes: You know what? That's my sister. My sister's at my mom's or my mom's at my sister's all the time. It's just everybody's different.

Me: *And that's a contributing factor in the research too.*

Jes: I bet! It's funny. Think about those quotes like, "It takes a village to raise a child." And it's true. And I think a lot of times from where I was and what I went through, I think I was too strong-willed of a person to ask for help. I'm not good at asking for help. I really didn't want anyone to see me struggle because I didn't want anyone to know I was having such a hard time. Because of pride or whatnot. Which is stupid. And that's another thing I'd tell my past self is "Drop your pride and ask for help. Because it's ok." Because you're right, it's a support system that's definitely needed.

So I started to see a psychologist and she said stop texting everyone and pick up the damn phone. And I need to call you more. This has been very nice.

Me: *And thank you so much. I know it's not an easy topic to talk about and I just think your perspective is going to be a solace to somebody who reads it. The solace to me, having experienced what I've experienced, is that maybe someone else can find some relief. So you will do that for somebody. And I hope that helps you.*

Chapter 29

Heather's Story

"I did, and still do, have a hard time balancing 'Mom-Heather' and

'Heather-Heather.'"

When Dan and I made the decision to build a house in Florida and leave LA, I was terrified to tell Heather and Jes. We had just found each other and I needed them. Our friendships were deep because of our circumstances, but they were also still new, less than a year old. Like our babies. And I was afraid that if they knew I was leaving, they'd start to withdraw. They wouldn't want to put in the effort because that easy camaraderie that came with our kids would be gone in a few short months. We put the deposit on the lot on New Year's Eve. We planned to leave LA by the Fourth of July. Why would they still want to hang out with me if I was going to be gone in six months? But of course I had to tell them so I steeled myself to the idea that they would gradually stop returning my calls. But the best thing happened. Instead of wanting to hang out less, they wanted to hang out more. They became determined to make the best of our last six months together and I was, and will always be, so grateful for their open hearts and arms.

Heather and I started spending nearly everyday together. Jes had a more complicated schedule, juggling work and school, so she wasn't always able to join us, but Heather and I had the random audition now and then to contend with. Otherwise we were full-time, stay-at-home moms: Sitting around in the morning, drinking coffee on the front stoop. Dragging kiddie pools into the backyard and eating popsicles. Going to libraries and museums around the city. We were game for anything and so were our kids. They became best little buds; I even wrote a little children's book that documented their adventures those last six months as a gift for Heather after we moved. Owen still likes to read that one.

Interviewing someone you feel very close to can sometimes be a challenge. I wanted to make sure you got to know her story without my "insider knowledge" influencing her answers or your perceptions, so I interviewed her as an impartial observer.

Here's our conversation, with my questions in bold.

* * * * *

What was your expectation of motherhood?

I had the typical "dream" motherhood in my head. I always had a dream of having a daughter with little blond curls, eating her ice cream cone as it was melting with the golden retriever running in the yard. I had this very idealistic vision that motherhood was just smooth and pretty and my children would be so easy and sweet and kind and gentle and loving. I mean, not easy [because] being an adult you see other moms and my mom . . . I saw my mom struggle a little. My sister was in high school when I was having my kids so I've watched my mom raise her basically, in my adult life, so I know the struggles are there but with my own self, I thought I could handle anything. I thought I was ready and prepared. But I wasn't.

What was your biggest fear about becoming a mother?

Losing control. Having something bigger and greater and more important than myself. I mean, I waited until I was 32 [to start a family] which I thought was plenty of time to get my own narcissistic pleasures out of the way. Especially, you know, being an actor and being in LA and it's all pretty much about you for a long time and I thought I had all the "me-me-me's" out of the way. I thought I was ready for somebody else and for something else, something bigger. So that was my fear, my fear was, "What's going to happen when it's not just me anymore?" The big fear of taking care of somebody else and knowing that the sole responsibility of their whole life is in your hands. And you don't realize until after you have the baby what a fragile little life that is. That first day they send you home and are like, "Here you go. All yours!" That's when it hits you, what a fragile life it is. So that was my fear, being in control of somebody else, other than myself. It's a huge responsibility and I haven't always been the best at responsibility in my life. Knowing that my greatest responsibility was coming was a pretty big fear.

Did you have an idea of how your labor would go?

You know it's funny because I grew up with panic attacks, um, pretty major ones and totally afraid of death. I lost my brother when I was 11, I lost a lot of family members right there after, just kind of boom boom boom in a row and it put a really big fear [in me] of hospitals and death and made me a hypochondriac, definitely. And I suffered from panic attacks for a very long time. So I was afraid of labor for a really long time. My focus was on the negative, of all the wrong things that could happen. I was pretty scared. Basically I was petrified of labor. Then I did some research and found a prenatal yoga class and was meditating, which helped with the panic attacks. And I had gotten some advice that, once I become a mother, that your motherly instinct kind of kicks in over your panic attacks and your anxiety and I kind of got it in my head that *maybe* my motherly instincts would take over. My yoga instructor was talking about her doula and I started researching doulas and what they did. And I kind of got it in my head that not only was I going to do this but I was going to be fine. And I don't know how and I don't know why because I was the most scared, probably, of labor, ever. And I just kind of completely turned it around to a more powerful, "I can do this, and I'm going to do it and I'm going to do it naturally and it's going to be fine and it's going to be great and nothing is going to go wrong." I just had to really, really keep telling myself that. That was kind of my vision: Nothing's going to go wrong, nothing's going to go wrong.

Did it live up to your expectations?

I think I got lucky. It wasn't easy. It wasn't short. It was 41 hours, which is crazy. It was way more intense than I could have ever imagined. And there were those moments of fear that I had envisioned. They did creep in. I had moments of total fear of, "Oh no, what's this? What's happening now?" I went into labor on Friday night at my house, and on Sunday after taking two doses of castor oil and vomiting and the contractions speeding up finally, we rushed to the hospital. And during transition, which we didn't know I was in transition, I mean, I took a birthing class. I knew that was supposed to be the most intense period, but nobody knew that I was there yet. And then I started to freak out. I started to have almost panic attack moments. It was so intense. I had been doing it for so long, so I was exhausted beyond. I felt like I was on an acid trip. I won't say why I know. I felt like I was floating in and out of reality and having freak out moments and needed to be grounded again. One of the nurses or somebody would say something or do something and put me back in my place. So it ended up being kind of crazy and way longer, but I did do what I set out to do which was to stay at home as long as possible. No drugs—without the assistance of Pitocin or anything and I felt fortunate that that happened. And the baby was healthy and great and that part lived up to my expectations. So there were some things that did live up to expectations and some that didn't, but overall I felt really happy with how it went.

What do you remember of those first moments holding your baby after birth?

I remember kind of this surreal feeling of, "What the fuck??" Everybody else is crying, my doula even is crying. My best friend was there; she was crying. My partner, he was crying. He was calling my parents on the phone and they were crying. And here I felt . . . that was one of those parts you envision, you envision this joy and complete and utter, sheer, biggest moment of joy. This just euphoric moment. But for me, I just felt . . . NOTHING. That makes me feel awful just to say that because here I am, I just had this incredible labor, just strong and "I did it." And now I'm holding this beautiful baby girl and she's crying and she's latching onto me and starting to nurse and everyone around me is so happy and so joyous and I was just . . . faking. I started faking it! I started going along with it. I started to cry. I *did* cry but they might have been tears of exhaustion and fear and there definitely was some joy in there but what I really felt like was, "What. Just. Happened." It was crazy and it was surreal and it was definitely NOT what I expected. I didn't expect to go through all that labor and have this beautiful baby put in my arms . . . actually, I helped pull her up. They didn't even put her in my arms! And I'm holding her there and I'm just like, "Oh my god." And I remember being wheeled down the hallway to my room and remember feeling like, "Is this real? Is this really happening? Did I just have a baby??"

I think we've seen a million movies on birth and we've kind of been shown that hospital scene when the husband passes out and everything kind of goes crazy in the hospital and then the baby is born and the husband and the wife are in ecstasy together and they're crying together and they're kissing and they're hugging. This moment, you know. And it happens. But that moment, reality just really sets in. And for the woman who has gone through hours and hours of excruciating pain and your body is just completely taxed and maxed out and all of sudden you get to that end point and you really have nothing left. You're spent. For me, by the time the baby got there, I felt like a shell of myself. I was laying there and I was holding her and I was happy, but I felt just like a shell. Those first hours just felt empty.

What was your biggest struggle as a new mother?

Balance, which I still struggle with now. I kind of chose a form of parenting that was all or nothing. Attachment parenting is what we chose to do. And I say "we" but I'm not sure Ted knew all that he was signing up for. Even in my early days, right from the get-go, I was nursing around the clock. I remember Ted's mom coming; she was here when I got home from the hospital. I remember not wanting to let her help me. I didn't want anyone else to help me. I didn't want her to hold the baby. I didn't want her to take the baby. I wanted to do it all. I wanted to have her [the baby] on me and beside me at all times. And even my doula came over to give me a post-natal massage to help my body get back and to help me sleep. I hadn't slept. Everybody kept telling me, "You have to sleep, you have to rest, you gotta sleep." And I had trouble with that. "I don't need sleep; my baby needs me." I would hear her cry and I couldn't sleep anyway. So I had a lot of trouble letting go of any responsibility and sharing responsibility with anybody else. Balancing that aspect. From there, I nursed, we co-slept, we still co-sleep, and I just kind of took on all of the responsibility and I don't let my partner take responsibility. I kind of took over everything with the baby. My motherly instinct was in full-force. I was an over-bearing mama bear. I had a really hard time. I did, and still do, have a hard time balancing "Mom-Heather" and "Heather-Heather." It's mostly all "mom-Heather," most of the time. It's maybe 5% "Heather-Heather" and 95% "Mom-Heather."

So then what would you say came most naturally? If that was the struggle, is it also part of what is natural?

Yeah. I feel motherhood comes naturally to me. I feel like I'm good at it. The people who are close to me say that I am good at it. I think my children are an example of how it does come naturally. But, yeah, I think that . . . I actually had a therapist tell me that there's a line where you go from being the "Excellent Mother" to being the

"Martyr." You can be "too good" of a mother. You go from doing it all to it becoming overbearing, over-controlling, too much. It's very natural to me, but it's also my struggle. My struggle is finding balance, when I see the moms that can do their business or still do what they were doing before or still manage to keep a somewhat normal sense of themselves "before-baby," that they still have that "after-baby." For me, I feel like I've come a long way. I'm far away from who I used to be. And maybe that's a good thing? I'm good at being a mom. I was meant to be a mom, but I always struggle with where does the mom-part stop, or where should it stop, and where should Heather also exist? How do the two of them co-exist?

What do you wish you had known before you gave birth?

How demanding it really was. How exhausting it really was —motherhood, early motherhood, the early stages, and motherhood in general. When I was really pregnant, I'd run into people on the street and they'd say, "Make sure you get those naps in while you can!" And you're like, "Yeah, hahaha" and you take all that stuff with a grain of salt and you don't realize, "No. They were serious." Like, get those naps in! Strangers would be like, "Make sure you go to the movies! Watch as many movies as you can!" And you'd be like, "What a weird thing to say to me. Like I'm not going to see movies anymore?" And then you have a baby and you're like, "I haven't seen a movie in a year." To watch award shows now just makes me sad because not only have I not seen the movies, but I don't know who some of these big actors are now. So yeah, there's nothing I would have done differently but I think I would have tried to be more mentally prepared for how tired [I'd be] and how exhausting and demanding motherhood is. I find that more so, now with the second, it doesn't come with the exhaustion of the baby, it comes with the exhaustion of keeping up with the toddler while you have the baby. The baby's easy. But I have more trouble with the three-nager that I'm struggling with.

If you could have a conversation with your pre-mom self, what advice would you give? All these people gave you advice, what would you say to yourself?

Go out dancing! Go stay out as late as you can and as much as you want. I'm in bed at 9pm every night now with my two and I have those moments of missing, not even just dancing or going out, but just staying up late with a good glass of wine and a girlfriend, just chitchatting and talking about nothing into the wee hours of the morning. I would say have more fun, don't worry about anything. Again, I waited until I was 32 to have a baby so I thought I had gotten all of that out! I did a pretty good job of living it up, I feel like I got all of that out of my system. But I guess you can never really get that out of your system. That's a thing that just stays with you. I think my pre-mom-self thought that once I became a mom, I wouldn't have those desires to do that stuff anymore. To go out dancing with my girlfriends, or whatever. I thought I would be pretty fine without any of it. But after being a mom now for 3.5 years, I miss those days. I miss those kinds of wild and carefree, don't-have-to-think-of-anyone-but-yourself moments. Now a mom of two, I'm just making sure everyone else is taken care of, constantly thinking about other people and it's wonderful and I wouldn't change it but there's something to be said about those wild and carefree nights. A girl never truly gets those dance parties out of her system. And I should be having dance parties in my living room! After the kids go to bed. And maybe one day I will.

Did you experience postpartum depression and/or anxiety? If yes, did you seek help? And did it help? And if you didn't seek help, why not? How were you able to cope?

With my first, I did not experience PPD. Anxiety, yes. It's in my nature. I had several moments of anxiety, almost-to-panic-attack status. And I think that all stemmed from lack of sleep and my system was just taxed. And I didn't have any help, no family in LA. It was rough, especially the first months. But that whole thing I was told about motherhood taking over anxiety . . . anytime I would start to have a panic attack, I would have that, "I can't have a panic attack because I have to be here for her" feeling. And it was this really weird shift. When I was 31, before I was a mother, there was nothing from stopping that panic attack from taking over my system. And now I had something much more important to override it. So it never got to that point.

But with my second one, actually, lately, he's 10 months and for the last, since he was about four months until now, I've definitely dealt with depression, anxiety, moments of just being completely overwhelmed. And just sad, frustrated, and angry. And I have a lot of really heavy emotions that have been pretty hard to deal with over the last couple of months. Those have also been compounded with a move across the country, having Ted travel all the time and being alone with both kids. [But] I feel like a lot of it is not circumstantial. All that doesn't help, but I think it also comes from my hormones not being fully ok after having my son. Just not being balanced mentally after the birth. With him, I had in the hospital . . . I had a lot of bleeding. I had a scary moment where I almost had to have a blood transfusion. I lost a lot of blood, I had to stay in the maternal ICU overnight. I had nobody that could stay with me in the hospital and it was a scary moment. That kind of pushed our move even quicker. Never really being able to kind of sit with your baby. With my first, I had a lot of moments of quiet and peace and just being with her. Getting a chance to sit and be still and be in the moment with her. And a lot of that helped me recover, my hormones and all of that stuff. With my second, right out of the get-go, when I got home from the hospital my older child had a fever and a virus. The day I got home, she was sick. And so it was out of the gate. And then the baby got a fever. So it was worrying is she ok? Is he going to be ok? She had to wear a mask. She wasn't allowed to be near him. Keeping the two separate—keeping your 2.5 year old away from her newborn brother and she was very attached to me and all of a sudden here's this new baby that's 100% dependent on me and at that point she was too. She's very attached. So I automatically felt completely pulled in multiple directions and didn't know quite how to handle that. And with that came a lot of guilt and sadness and anxiety. That caused a lot of anxiety for me, not knowing how to do both really well. That coming right off of a birth, I felt down and way overwhelmed. And way unable to handle what was going on and I feel like from that moment I've just been playing catch up. I never got those moments with my second, to just kind of be and stare into his eyes and lay and take a nap with him and just be quiet and calm. To kind of let my mind just sit and rest and recover. Because now if he's asleep, she's awake. If she's awake, he's asleep. So now, my brain just never gets a moment's peace or rest. And that causes anxiety and has caused depression. And I haven't gotten any help yet. I haven't gotten any treatment yet. I just keep thinking, "It's going to get better, it's going get better. It's going to work itself out." And it probably will eventually. But it could get worse. I could get crazier before it gets better, I honestly don't know. My son is about to walk any day now, so I think sometimes, maybe then it'll be better . . .

So how are you coping? Are you coping at this point? Or are you just getting by, day-by-day?

I'm coping the best that I can. I have moments of complete breakdowns, where I say, "I can't do this, I can't handle this, I don't know." My daughter is a highly sensitive, very intelligent, extremely sensitive and she's going through a lot of things. So where the two would be a lot to handle anyway because of the stages that they're in . . . intellectually I have to be in both places, emotionally I have to be in both places and then, on top of that, my daughter is going through some things that make the transitions of the day very difficult. I find myself getting angry a lot. I never thought of myself as an angry person. It used to take a lot for me to get to a snapping point, before I would really lose my temper. And now it feels like my fuse has become way shorter, as a mom now, with the second. The patience I had with the first one, I feel like I have half that amount of that patience now. And of course that brings guilt, always questioning yourself. Are you doing this right? Are you scarring your children if you yell at them? We get bombarded with, "Time outs are good." "Time outs are bad." "Spanking is ok." "Spanking will scar your child for life." I'm constantly looking for a way to manage, with a way to deal with my emotions, my daughter's emotions, the needs of my young son. And I'm trying so hard to deal with all of them. And I don't get any time to focus on one at a time. Constantly dealing with a multitude of people's emotions. And then you're like, "Oh yeah, my partner's emotions." There are emotions there. So it's A LOT. And it's difficult and I find it very challenging. I definitely have moments. I have those just breakdown and cry moments. And I have those now and I feel like I haven't had those in a really long time. Whether that's depression or I just feel like I'm completely overwhelmed. Those moments of feeling like I just can't handle it. Those moments make me burst into tears.

Motherhood is crazy.

Motherhood can make you crazy. That's very true.

I'm trying not to get to that point. I was home [visiting my mom] last week and I think my daughter had a moment and I yelled at her and then I cried. And I told my mom [that] I felt bad. And my mom was like, "You are incredibly patient. I wouldn't be that patient." And I told her, "Mom, I just feel like I'm on the edge. I don't know how much, I just feel I'm so overwhelmed." My grandmother had a full on breakdown, like a nervous breakdown, when my mother was 11. And it was just, she had been broken down; over she couldn't handle being a mom. And she was a mom of four. And it just little by little took its toll. And you look at that and you think, "I don't want to get to that point." How do I not get to *that* point? How do I carve out time? Everyone says you have to make time for yourself. But how? There's not enough time in the day to have time to myself. It's amazing that some women can do it but we're not in a place, where I can get it very easily. I mean, meditating? I've meditated for five years and I don't even do that now. I find it hard to find twenty minutes, you know? But then I look at someone else like my dad's mother who literally had 10 kids, back to back to back, and she was totally fine. She had ten! And they were like a year apart. She had no nervous breakdown. You'd think you'd have a nervous breakdown with ten, not four. So you think, how in the world did you have *ten?* And you didn't lose your mind? And here I am, I've only got two. Why am I struggling so much with two? How can I not find the balance? What am I doing wrong? It's mindboggling. That's stressful. Why is this so difficult for me?

Chapter 30

Emily's Story

"Having a baby and working full time outside the home presented

more logistical turmoil than I had ever anticipated."

Emily and I are friends because our husbands have been friends since high school. Dan is one of those guys who believes in "quality over quantity" and I've been the beneficiary of that philosophy. Good people find good people and as a result, I've had the pleasure of getting to know Emily, Steve's wife. She is originally from California and she went to college out east where she met Steve. They've lived on a boat, they've lived in Steamboat, CO, and now they're raising their family in their beautiful home in Southern California, just a two-hour drive down from where we lived in LA.

The summer I found out I was pregnant with Owen, we met up in Anaheim to go to an Orioles-Angels game. We had dinner first and neither of us was drinking, but we didn't pry. As soon as Dan and I were in the car after the game, we were like, "I bet they're pregnant, too!" But since we were waiting to tell friends, we understood if they wanted to wait as well. And sure enough, our due dates were six weeks apart. So it came as a big surprise to everyone when Baby Olivia decided to make her debut three weeks after Owen was born. Emily has one of the craziest birth stories to share. It is the exact opposite of mine. It involves going into labor in the morning while at work as a teacher, going home and finishing up lesson plans for the substitute teacher taking over while she was on maternity leave (she thought she'd have more time to complete them!), then getting stuck in rush hour traffic, on a Friday, in San Diego. This meant driving on the shoulder, hoping to get stopped by a cop. She didn't have such luck. She ended up transitioning in the car and giving birth within moments of arriving at the hospital. I'm stressed just typing it all out.

I remember seeing a picture of Steve and Emily out to dinner with Olivia, in an actual restaurant, a week after she was born. I had no joy for them. I was pissed. I was four weeks postpartum at that point and still had trouble walking. I had just started sleeping in our bed again, instead of the rocker-recliner. The idea of being out in the world was still far from my thoughts and I couldn't believe that she felt well enough to go out to eat. I was still having trouble eating at home. Oh, hello Depression. I recognize you now. At the time, I didn't though. I just felt anger. I chalked it up to having a caesarean, rather than a vaginal birth. Floating along in my depression, I was unable to recognize that Emily was having her own difficulties, ones I couldn't see in a snapshot from a restaurant. I just saw that she was happy. And that just magnified that I was not. I've said it before and I'll say it again: Pictures lie! And by "lie," I mean that they don't always tell the whole truth.

Here's Emily story, in her own words.

* * * * *

"Transitioning" Back to Work

I was filled with dread as my nine-week maternity leave came to an end. The day before I went back to work was a grim one. I cried on and off throughout the day. I couldn't believe that some people actually had to return to work at 6 weeks. I remember saying out loud to a friend, "This is a form of cruel and unusual punishment." I hadn't been separated from my precious baby girl for more than an hour or so since her birth, and now I was about to commute 45 minutes, work for 8 hours, and then come home. It felt like Day One of what was going to be the rest of my life, and it felt horrible.

My "transition" back to work felt more like doing a polar bear plunge from my current life as a new mom to a full-time-crazy-person; commuting/working/pumping/ commuting/working/pumping-repeat. It was a complete emotional slap in the face. I was exhausted and overwhelmed. I cried in the car to work most days, and

Olivia screamed during the commute home. There's nothing like being trapped in your car in bumper-to-bumper traffic with a baby screaming at the top of her lungs in the car seat. "Only 45 minutes until we're home . . . !" Sometimes I would actually lean against the steering wheel, plug my ears with my fingers and drive with my elbows . . . 5 miles per hour.

After Olivia was born, it became clear that we were having difficulty with breastfeeding. She wasn't able to latch on. When she was a few days old, the lactation specialist said that she had a tongue-tie, which is very common. We continued to struggle with feeding for another two weeks. We finally made it to the appointment with the doctor to have the tie clipped. I heard from so many people that everything becomes much easier once this simple procedure is done. I couldn't wait. After a thorough examination, the doctor shared that her tongue-tie was too far back in her mouth to be removed or clipped. The only way to strengthen her latch and make her sucking reflex stronger was to continue the practice of breastfeeding, and by doing little exercises with my finger in her mouth. I was disappointed. Long story short, Olivia never fully developed a strong latch until she was several months old . . . like 5 months old. Feeding her was always a challenge and most often a scene. This was how I spent my down time.

Other highlights of returning to work include locking my office door during my 20-minute lunch and posting a sign on the outside that read, "Please come back later." I guess it wasn't clear enough, because while trying to eat and pump at the same time I still got walked in on. Twice! I had to create my own personal form of a "duck and cover" drill. Earthquakes? No problem. Someone walking in on you pumping? That's life or death! I've never dove under a desk for shelter faster than when I realized someone was unlocking that door.

Having a baby and working full time outside the home presented more logistical turmoil than I had ever anticipated. I was trapped by the schedule of the day care.

Gone were the days of arriving early/leaving early, arriving

late/leaving late. It was 7-5 sharp . . . right in time for rush

hour traffic. I soon realized that the schedule was not feasible

or reasonable to sustain, but one that only fostered stress,

anxiety, and a feeling of pure exhaustion. The 48-hour

weekends felt like cruel jokes; I most often had to work for a

few hours then as well. I was so tired, I couldn't really enjoy

them. People kept saying, "It will get easier. It will get

better." But I knew in my gut that I needed to do something

more drastic and make a change.

This became my new mission. I knew I

couldn't continue on in survival mode, and I wanted to be

happy and balanced. I wanted to enjoy being a mom, but I

still knew that I had to work full time to help support my

family financially. As tough as the job search is, I started it.

Resume, online applications, interviews, credential checks,

constant scouring of openings. After a year, I was able to land a job in a district close to my home, allowing Olivia to attend a daycare only minutes away. My husband now does the drop offs, and I do the pick-ups. I spent some time in therapy, just processing what I had been through and trying to clear my head. My therapist told me that I had signs of Post-Traumatic Stress Disorder (PTSD). I was shocked at first to hear that, but it actually made a lot of sense. Talking this through with a professional, and being able to take the time to actually go to these appointments was immensely helpful.

Currently my days are still long, but I'm in a good place. I feel balanced. Olivia is almost two years old now, and I'm starting to feel "normal." I'm starting to feel a deep sense of joy that I didn't even know I had lost. I can say, right at this moment, that I am truly happy.

Chapter 31

Michaela's Story

"It'd be Pleasantville. I wasn't aware that anything would be

difficult."

I've dogged on social media a bit throughout this book mainly because I think getting caught up in carefully curated online personas can be dangerous. Mostly because I get caught up and also carefully curate all the dang time. With that said, social media does have its benefits, like keeping people connected who may otherwise lose touch. I met Michaela in an acting class. We were assigned to do a scene together, which meant a lot of rehearsals outside of class. We got along great and we worked hard on our scene and then . . . we never put it up. She was starting nursing school and was getting married soon and ended up leaving the class. That would normally be a very frustrating scenario because of all the work we put into it; never getting to perform it would seem like a waste. But at that point I considered Michaela a friend and was happy for all the changes headed her way. We became Facebook friends and a couple of years passed.

When I was pregnant I made a little announcement about it on ye ol' Facebook and she reached out. She was so excited for me. She, too, had recently become a mother. She had also done her OBGYN/Labor and Delivery rotation at the hospital where I was delivering. She told me if I wanted to chat at some point and ask questions, she'd love to connect. Why, yes! Yes, I would like to pick your brain a bit. I was all about collecting information during those pregnancy months. I was a hoarder of information. And so we talked on the phone for over an hour while I took notes. And then we went our separate ways again, until after Owen was born. And I was like . . . WHAT-IS-GOING-ON-THIS-IS -THE-WORST. She was one of the few already-established friends I had who was also a mother. So we reconnected. I'll never forget going to her house, sitting on her couch while Owen and her daughter played, and hearing all about how hard new motherhood was for her, too. And she was already pregnant with her next child! That blew my mind. Having another child was not something I was sure I'd ever want with how I was feeling. But she had felt the despair in the beginning, too. Not to the point where she sought medical treatment but she knew how hard it all was. *And she was willing to do it all again.* It gave me hope. And it still does.

This is Michaela's story, as told to me through an interview.

* * *

What was your expectation for motherhood?

I was going to have a baby, go back to work after 6 weeks, the baby was going to sleep for long intervals and would quickly and easily take to a bottle. I would just bake cookies all day. It'd be Pleasantville. I wasn't aware that anything would be difficult. Because I just graduated nursing school, I thought lack of sleep would be nothing. It was 10 1/2 months before I was able to go back to work.

Did you have a romanticized notion of being a mom?

Yes! I thought it was going to be easy. All my friends who had kids only glamorized it. The only negative thing I heard was, "Get enough sleep now."

What was your biggest fear about becoming a mom?

Getting older and having regrets about not pursuing my dreams before entering into motherhood. Since I had given up acting and put everything into nursing school, I didn't want to feel like I set my dreams aside again. I was afraid that this time my dreams might not be there to come back to, as Hollywood has a youthful reputation.

What do you remember from those first moments of holding your baby after birth?

The sex of the baby was a surprise, but after no sleep, I was delirious. After giving birth my doctor held the baby up and said "Look it's a girl!" "Yay. I'm so happy. Can I have some food now?" I was so thirsty and hungry. Due to the small diameter in the baby's umbilical cord, her initial assessment took longer than usual. This gave me time to regroup. I was so exhausted. With my second delivery, the baby was out in two pushes, so instead of feeling exhausted at the end of labor, I still had a significant amount of energy left. The two experiences, with how different the labors were, made such a difference with how those first moments after delivery were.

What was your biggest struggle as a new mom?

Breastfeeding. In nursing school, I shadowed a lactation nurse and I learned how to help postpartum patients nurse. So I thought I knew what to do. This is why I made the decision not to take a breastfeeding class. Because my baby did not latch, I was told by the postpartum nurse to feed my baby with a syringe. This continued at home for 2 weeks. At her 2-week check up, a lactation nurse was recommended and she came to my house. The lactation nurse was able to get my baby to latch on immediately. And then, I literally did not leave the house for 6 months. My baby ate nonstop, only breaking to sleep. While awake, she screamed nonstop if she was not eating. To this day, she still has a big appetite. My second child latched immediately, and eats every 3-4 hours. A very different experience than it was with my first child.

What came the most naturally?

Safety. Because of nursing school, and all the research I did prior to motherhood, I had a low level of anxiety going into motherhood. My nursing background gave me the confidence to be able to care for my baby, but to also know when to call the pediatrician.

What do you wish you had known before you gave birth?

I wish I knew I could afford to hire help, even if it was only for 4 hours a week. Just so I could take a shower or whatever. I hired help for the second child.

If you could have a conversation with your pre-mom-self, what piece of advice would you give?

Take a breastfeeding class! And before deciding on a class, find out the credentials of the person who will be teaching the class.

The lactation nurse I chose for myself was an RN who had 30 years of hospital experience.

When you went back to work after maternity leave, what was the hardest adjustment? And what was the best thing about going back to work?

My child was 10 1/2 months old before I went back to work. She had never taken to a bottle, and now she was going to have no choice but to take to the bottle if she wanted any milk throughout the day. I was so excited to be back at work, but my breasts were so engorged, and it was painful. At the time, I was unaware there were handheld pumps and I'd have 12-hour shifts on set (*she works as the on-set nurse for a reality television show*). There was nowhere on-set, except maybe the bathroom, I could go to relieve the pressure. That was hard. Best thing? Freedom. Being able to eat a full meal without interruption, having adult conversations, and just being able to sit and not have the responsibility of watching and caring for a baby.

Did you experience postpartum depression and/or anxiety?

No. I was just exhausted. My first child ate for 48 hours straight one time. I cried from exhaustion. I was just really tired, and that was really difficult. Although medical professionals say it's safe, I chose not to drink anything with caffeine in it during my pregnancy and while I was breastfeeding. I had a few friends who formula fed, and I was so envious because they would often post pictures of themselves on Facebook drinking a large cup of coffee. I was aggravated they were so chipper, and I was so exhausted. But I had come across a webpage that discussed, week-by-week, the benefits a baby receives from breastfeeding. I can't remember where I saw it. Pinterest? KellyMom? "I prevent asthma because I breastfed." [It said] things like that. After having done a pediatrics rotation, I was terrified that something would go wrong, so I wanted to do my best to lessen any risk.

Final thoughts?

Not all women fall in love with their babies right after giving birth! Expectations of mother's are so high. After giving birth, people would say to me, "Aren't you just in love with her?" In my head I was thinking, "In love? No, not really? I don't even know this person." And it was true. Falling in love with my baby took time. I had to get to know her. She had to get to know me. We had to work together and DEVELOP our bond. And she was a challenging baby, and I was always exhausted, so it wasn't a quick and easy process. But everyday that bond strengthened, and I love that I allowed myself to let that love develop naturally over time. I am thankful that I had the courage not to force it just because it's expected that a new mom should instantly love her baby. I even had doubts during my second pregnancy. I thought, "How is there any more room in my heart to love another child?" By this time, the amount of love I had developed for my first child was so great, that I was scared I would not have any left over to give to another child. But I was wrong. I gave birth to my second child, and this time, I fell instantly in love. See this time around, I was aware of how wonderful it is and how blessed I am to be a mother.

Chapter 32

Fahey's Story

"I really didn't expect it to take over my whole life 24/7."

Dan's parents are storytellers. Dan would say they always tell the same ten stories over and over and I wouldn't disagree. But what I love is how when we visit, we eat dinner, clean up and then end up sitting at the dining room table talking for hours after. There are usually snacks in the center of the table and we nibble our way through the night, telling stories we've heard before and discovering new ones. Sometimes we discover new details to the well-trodden stories, but it's remarkable to me how consistent the narrative usually is.

One of their favorite tales is about Dan's mom, Fahey, soon after her first son Jeremy was born. They laugh about how hard a time she had at first. Through laughter, Joe will say, "I came home and thought Jeremy was dead. I walked in the door and Fahey was sitting on the couch, sobbing uncontrollably, and the baby was completely still in her arms. But she was crying so hard I didn't realize he was just asleep." And then Fahey will chime in and explain, "He had been crying nonstop all day and he had finally stopped. And so then *I* started crying." And they laugh about how hysterical she got and how it must have looked to Joe, walking in after being gone all day. And we would laugh along with them, before we had a child of our own, and shake our heads at "how crazy" that must have been.

Then I had Owen. And that story stopped being a lighthearted recollection of early motherhood. I knew that hysterical cry well. And I realized what was really going on in the subtext of that story.

Here's Fahey's story, in her own words.

* * *

"Eventually It Became Easier . . ."

When Owen was 5 months old, we did a road trip with Dan, Meagan, Owen, and our other two granddaughters to see the Sequoias. Owen did great and Meagan seemed happy to be there with us. I never noticed anything after that nor did Dan mention anything when we spoke. Meagan seemed to be doing very well and was just so happy to have Owen with her. I never suspected she was still suffering from depression, nor how bad she was really feeling. I feel a little guilty now because I should have known or at least talked to her about how she was feeling since the birth. We didn't really talk about it much but when we did, she didn't "fall apart" – just listened and spoke occasionally. If I could go back, I would definitely talk to Meagan alone and ask how was she really *feeling, especially since I had gone through postpartum depression myself.*

No matter how much you read or talk to people about having children, you won't understand until you "live" it. All my life, the only thing I really wanted was to be married and have children. When I got pregnant with our first child, we couldn't have been happier. My pregnancy was ideal—no problems with retaining fluid, gaining too much weight, not being able to sleep at night, etc. The baby was very active but didn't keep me awake at night. The delivery went off perfectly and I delivered a 9 lb 1 oz baby boy. He was beautiful. I couldn't wait for them to bring him to my room. He began nursing immediately and after nursing for 20 minutes, took a 4 oz bottle of sugar water. I did not realize at the time this would be a problem. When we went home, he was nursing every two hours and I was sore—to the point it was painful when he latched on. He cried almost constantly because he was hungry. I just couldn't keep up with it so I discontinued nursing and started him on a bottle. This made me feel unfit as a mother—I couldn't even feed my own baby!

*When you find out you are pregnant, you read books and talk to people about what to do and not to do during your pregnancy. They tell you what to expect from the baby at monthly intervals. They tell you to get lots of rest. But nobody tells you how **you** are going to feel. You are tired all the time, your hormones are going crazy, you are sore from the delivery (whether it be cesarean or vaginal birth). You want to rest but you can't because every time the baby makes a sound you are worried that something is wrong. Nobody tells you, "Your life will never be the same again." You are now at the mercy of a tiny, dependent person whom you love. If you are used to having a schedule – forget it! The baby makes the schedule. These are all things you know before you have a baby, but it isn't "real" until the baby is there. I believe this is why I was depressed for a while after having my first child. I really didn't expect it to take over my whole life 24/7. Eventually it became easier —we got used to the baby's schedule.*

It wasn't until Dan & Meagan were with us for Christmas that Meagan told me about her depression since the birth of Owen. I was really surprised. Nothing she did or said in the last few months would have led me to believe this was the case. I told her she was a really good actress—I did not detect a thing.

Chapter 33

Tell Your Story

I used the same set of writing prompts when talking to my fellow mamas included here in this book. I sent this set of questions ahead of time and let them know that they could use them as a jumping off point to tell a specific aspect of their story or, if they preferred, I could interview them using these questions line-by-line. The decision was up to them. I've included those same writing prompts here so that when you're ready to tell your story, you can use them as a guideline, too. Whether you're like me and have postpartum depression as a diagnosed illness or you're like so many women I know who struggle but don't seek help, these questions are here to help you sort through your journey. And it's a journey, man.

As I type this, I'm nearly three years into this motherhood gig and I'm still shifting and adjusting and learning and balancing and rebalancing. And I'm able to do that and be the mother my son needs me to be, and the person I need me to be, because I sought help, went on medication and recalibrated. That's what *I* needed. What *you* need may be different. My biggest hope is that you find out what you need and take the steps to get it.

There is hope.

You are not alone.

You are stronger than you know.

* * * * *

Writing Prompts

- What was your expectation for motherhood?

- Did you have a romanticized notion of being a mom?

- What was your biggest fear about becoming a mom?

- Did you have an idea of how you wanted your labor to go?

- How did you prepare for your labor? Classes/doula/etc.?

- Did it go that way?

- What do you remember from those first moments of holding your baby after birth?

- What was your biggest struggle as a new mom?

- What came the most naturally?

- What do you wish you had known before you gave birth?

- What do you wish you could have been more relaxed about post-birth, looking back?

- If you could have a conversation with your pre-mom-self, what piece of advice would you give?

- If you went back to work after maternity leave, what was the hardest adjustment? What was the best thing about going back to work? If given the option, would you want to be a stay-at-home mom?

- If you became a stay-at-home mom, what was the hardest adjustment? What was the best thing about staying at home? If given the option, would you want to "go back to work"?

- Did you experience postpartum depression and/or anxiety? If yes, did you seek help? And did it help? If you didn't seek help, why not? How were you able to cope?

Epilogue

One

She turns one this month, but it feels like she has already reached that milestone. She started walking at nine-months-old, a full month and a half before her brother started. Her fine motor skills surprise us everyday, the way she holds a crayon to scribble or picks up a piece of lint off of the floor to put in her mouth before I can swat it away. She imitates words and sounds like she knows what she's saying. I swear she said 'wheelbarrow' when we were outside playing in the driveway a month ago. Her first word was also 'ball,' like her brother, but she's been saying it for two months now. He waited until the day after his first birthday party to say it. I don't mean to compare and contrast but it's hard not to when he's all I've known. And now she's here and different, and yet the same, simultaneously.

After I lost the baby in the summer of 2015, I wasn't quite sure I'd want to try again. I wasn't sure I would even be able to get pregnant. I started doing ovulation kits, looking for a smiley face that would tell me when we should have sex. We'd try and no luck. The end of the year was approaching and we decided if we weren't pregnant by the end of the year then we'd take a break, maybe talk to a specialist at some point. Or maybe not. We decided we were okay being the parents to one beautiful child.

I was doing the ovulation tests in the mornings, like the instructions suggested. I was certain I should be ovulating but I wasn't. It was a Tuesday and I was teaching music class. After class, I was speaking with one of the mothers who asked if she could talk to me about something personal. She knew I had a son about her son's age and no other children. She wanted to know if that was by choice or by chance. She had been trying to have another child and was having a difficult time conceiving. She was looking for an ally and she found one.

I gave her the brief summary of our journey (PPD, miscarriage, fertility issues) and told her how I was certain I was supposed to be ovulating like, today, but that I wasn't. I shared my theory that maybe something got botched in my surgery over the summer. This was where my mind was at. She asked how many times a day I was doing the test strips and I told her once every 24-hours, like the instructions say. "Oh, I test three times a day," she responded. It never crossed my mind to test more than once. So that evening I tested again. Smiley face, where there had been nothing that morning. I told Dan it was now or never. I tested again the next morning and, sure enough, no smiley face. If it wasn't for my conversation after class, Quinn wouldn't be here about to celebrate her first birthday.

When I found out I was pregnant I had a very different reaction than times past. I wasn't happy. I wasn't excited. I was numb. I was scared. And then I had a full blown panic attack. What was I thinking trying to have another child? What if I got sick again? Owen was potty-trained, he was becoming more independent everyday, we didn't have to lug a stroller everywhere because he could actually walk alongside me and hold my hand. He listened, he was cautious, he could tell me if he was hungry or tired or mad. I was going to start all over again? I had (barely) gotten us through those first tough years, I had written a book about it, I was on the other side and had finally found a sense of balance. This was the dumbest thing I had ever done. So I cried hard, shared my fears with Dan, and called my psychiatrist.

I explained my anxieties and she asked, "But what if it's *not*? What if it's not as hard as before? What if you don't get sick? What if the baby is easy? What if you are more able? Why does it have to be the worst outcome that you fear instead of the positive outcome that you look forward to?" She explained that looking for all the negative outcomes wasn't being a realist, it was being a depressive. And that it's ok to consider the positive possibilities. It doesn't make you naive or unprepared but it does make you happier in the here and now, which is all we really have control of anyway. The skeptic in me was resistant to shifting my perspective. I didn't want to set myself up for such a big fall again.

Only, I didn't have to fall into an abyss again. I knew where the bottom was. I'd been there, face down, under the water, unsure of how to surface. And I survived. And I'd survive again. Instead of worrying about all the things that could go wrong, I could prepare this time so that I could swim.

I decided to go on a low dose of Zoloft as soon as the baby was born. I didn't want to wait to see if I started to feel dark and then have to wait another few weeks for the medication to start working. That made me nervous. It felt important to take a preemptive strike, especially given the anxieties I was already facing.

My family, bless them. They all asked, "How can we make this better this time? Tell us where to be and we'll be there." So my parents and my brother and his wife were at my house the night before I was scheduled to deliver. It felt like we were celebrating a holiday. Greg and Stephanie took care of Owen while my parents came to the hospital with us. After Quinn was born, my mom stayed two and half weeks to help out. Then Dan's parents came to relieve her and they stayed another two weeks. Knowing that I was going to have a month solid of live-in help eased my anxieties further. It was a luxury that they were all able to pitch-in in that way and I'll be forever humbled and grateful that they did.

I was nervous throughout the pregnancy that I would lose this baby too. I didn't talk about it much but it was always there, just under the surface, until the moment she was born.

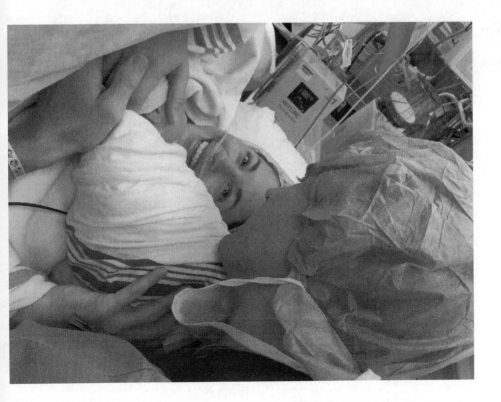

And the moment she was born? Talk about night and day experiences. My anesthesiologist this time was a man named Tom, who asked Dan for his phone right before the baby was delivered. He said he'd take a few pictures for us. It wasn't until a few days

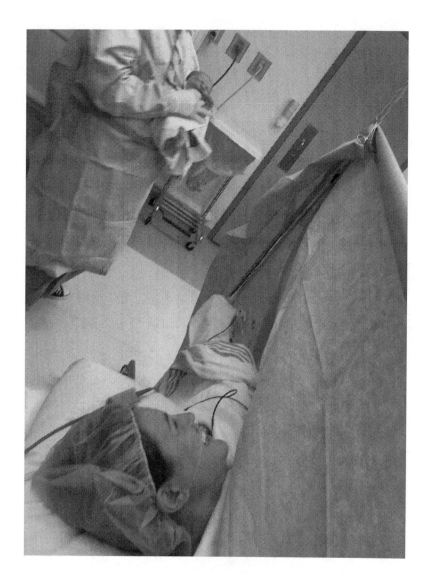

later that we even discovered the pictures and it was like we had hired a lifestyle photographer to be in the delivery room.

The smile was real this time. The tears were of joy.

Having these pictures healed me in a way that surprised me. He also captured the actual moment she emerged from my belly, beyond the sheet. I was worried that seeing the surgery would be difficult to process, especially since I had longed for a natural delivery with Owen and hadn't even been able to look at my caesarean scar until a full year after he was born. But it wasn't difficult to look at. In fact, it was like rewriting the script of all that went wrong with Owen's delivery. It felt like a correction. Suddenly I could appreciate all that I couldn't see or feel three and half years prior. I couldn't go back and change Owen's delivery but I could appreciate the miracle of it more now that I had this delivery to see and feel. It felt full circle. In the picture above, I'm saying to Dan, "We did it."

She was here. We were ok. We were all going to be ok.

We did it.

Acknowledgements

Thank you to the amazing women who shared their stories here with me and with you.

Thank you Michaela, Jes, Heather, and Emily, not only for contributing but for being friends without whom that first year would have been unnavigable.

Thank you Fahey for remembering and relating.

Thank you Mom for your unconditional love and for always being my safe place to land.

Thank you Kelsey for your dedication to this book as my cover artist, sounding board, and seestra.

Thank you Stephanie for your feedback and your cheerleading.

Thank you Dad for always encouraging me to write and dream big.

Thank you Abi for sharing your insight as a doctor and a friend.

Thank you Erin C. for volunteering to read through my first rough draft and giving insightful feedback when this book was just a baby.

Thank you Silissa for sharing your industry know-how and connecting me to Laura.

Thank you Laura Chasen for embracing, editing, and making this book work better than I could have on my own.

Thank you Finding Time to Read Book Club for always asking when you could read my book and actually meaning it.

Thank you Kristen, Brie, and Pam for your mad proofreading skills. Any errors still remaining are totally my fault. Bonus for you, dear reader, if you found any.

Thank you Alex at Cedars Sinai & Tom at Baptist South, for bringing humanity to your job.

Thank you Brooke Shields for sharing your story so I felt less alone.

Thank you Dan for holding us together and for being the husband and the father our family needs.

Above all, thank you Owen and Quinn for giving me life.

Now What?

A Resource Guide

Since becoming a mom in 2013, postpartum conditions have become more mainstream to talk about. There are blogs like Scary Mommy (www.scarymommy.com), that often have pieces that take the sheen off of motherhood a bit and bring things back to reality. There's Bunmi Laditan (www.instagram.com/bunmiladitan), who has been so open and honest with her mental health struggles and how they've intersected with her motherhood experience. Celebrities like Chrissy Teigen, Kristen Bell, Hayden Panettiere, and Gwyneth Paltrow have come forward and talked at a very public level about the very private experience of postnatal mental health issues. I've seen the topic tackled on some of my favorite shows, like *Blackish* and *Nashville*. PPD and beyond is being talked about. Yes!

Yet even with the increased visibility of this topic by our culture as a whole, it is still a sensitive and very personal thing to navigate when you are in the midst of it. My hope is that by sharing my story, my friends' stories, and the following resources, anyone that is still struggling can find their way back to themselves. Back to the mother they always thought they'd someday be. Back to a place of health. Back to reality. Because the truth is, depression lies. Here's a few places to go that can help you see the truth.

* * * * *

Postpartum Support International

www.postpartum.net

From their website: "We provide direct peer support to families, train professionals, and provide a bridge to connect them." Their website is a treasure trove of resources and information, including tangible ways to find help in your own community. They have chapters throughout the US and in 36 countries around the world. This is a great place to start.

EDINBURGH POSTNATAL DEPRESSION SCALE (EPDS)

At Quinn's 6-week check-up, her pediatrician gave me a clipboard with ten questions on it. It was a mental health checklist called the Edinburgh Postnatal Depression Scale. This was not given to me three and a half years earlier at Owen's 6-week check-up. I wish it had been. If your doctor doesn't give you this, it's easy enough to find online. Just search the name to find PDF versions or go to https://psychology-tools.com/epds/ for a self-scoring version. I did a practice test on how I would have likely answered after Owen was born and it scored me as "generally indicative of depression." That could have been my wakeup call.

Your Medical Insurance

It's the way I found my therapist and it's as good a place as any to start. Search providers near you for both psychologists and psychiatrists. Talk to your OB/GYN or general practitioner to see if they have therapists they refer their patients to. If you don't have someone in your life you feel comfortable asking for a mental health care professional recommendation, chances are the medical professionals can point you in the right direction.

What do you say?

I called several therapists before I found the one I wanted to go to. I asked each office, *"Does the doctor specialize in postpartum issues?"* It felt important to me to have someone that did. I also confirmed that they still took my insurance! Don't forget to cover that base.

* * * * *

Good luck out there, Warriors. Whether you're finding help for yourself, your wife, your sister, your friend - there IS help to be found.

And where there is help, there is *hope*.

Made in the USA
Columbia, SC
22 December 2019